PORTRAIT

OF A BANK ROBBER

Daniel Killion
with Matthew Klane

Cover and Interior Design by
Vinnie Corbo and Matthew Klane

Volossal
Publishing

Published by Volossal Publishing
www.volossal.com

Copyright © 2023
ISBN 979-8-9877903-4-2

CONTENTS

PROTEST CENTRAL
July 2020

I was driving to see my daughter on the other side of town. Approaching an intersection, I slowed down, but then I accelerated as the light turned green. I didn't even have that oh-shit-I'm-about-to-be-in-a-car-accident moment. Nah. Never saw it coming.

The next thing I remember is waking up in a hospital bed. My brain was... broken. No memories at all of what happened. Rosemarie had to tell me the story: "Danny, you were hit by a police car on his way to a call. He ran through the red light, plowed right into your van, just behind your driver's side door." And then she told me, you know, how she had told me this story already. Probably 70 times in the last seven hours.

It was a complete fucking nightmare. Afterwards, I thought, "Everything will be fine." The police would pay for my van and cover my hospital bills. Or maybe I'd even sue and receive a big chunk of money. But, so far, that hasn't been the case. Instead, the city blamed *me*. They waited a week to issue a ticket. "Failure to yield to an emergency vehicle." And then sued *my* insurance company, $26,000, to replace their SUV.

That was January 11th. More than a month later, I was still having residual symptoms from the concussion. Fog. Depression. My knee was pretty jacked up. After realizing that the police were trying to fuck me over, we consulted a lawyer-friend to see if I had any recourse. I just felt so frustrated, and angry, and confused. Rosemarie would catch me crying randomly around the house. Breaking down.

We were deep into February by the time life gradually began to feel somewhat normal again. But then March hit, you know, and the world imploded.

*

Learning to live with the new reality of COVID-19 has been pretty bizarre. To say the least. Nothing is normal. You always feel wobbly. Like you can't get your feet underneath you. And Florida just had 15,000 new cases *yesterday*, so it's not going away anytime soon. Within that first month alone, I probably lost out on $5,000 in retail sales. It hurts. I'm not going to lie. But I try to keep perspective. The company losing money isn't that big of a deal compared to the fact that *people are dying*.

The company: Weathered Wood. We've been in business for over eight years now. Before that, I was just a commercial carpenter, you know, a pull-my-oar kind of a guy. Woke up every morning. Went to my construction job. But, man, I fucking hated it. While I was incarcerated, I had spent a lot of my time making art. So then, on the outside, I desperately wanted to be involved in something like that again and potentially even make an income from my creativity.

When I moved to this area, after getting off work, I would walk along the Hudson River and hunt for cool shit. Especially driftwood. I'd find so many amazing and unique pieces. Many times, they were art in-and-of-themselves. At first, I would just mount the coolest pieces on a board, but then started making stuff with the driftwood. Little abstract sculptures. Mirrors, lamps, arbors, horses. Pretty soon, I was selling my stuff around town out of other people's little retail stores.

At my construction sites, after remodeling a structure, I also noticed how they often threw the original lumber into dumpsters. And some of the structures in this area are fucking *old*, you know, built between 1850-1890. So I'd dumpster-dive. Take this history-rich lumber, reclaim it, and turn it into furniture. One-of-a-kind pieces that you can't find at Pottery Barn. Eventually, we were doing so well selling furniture, I thought, "Why don't we just get our own store?"

The store is in downtown Troy, NY. One of the tri-cities of the Capital District. Albany, Schenectady, *Troy*. The home of Uncle Sam. Haha. At one point in history, because of its proximity to the river, and location between New York City and the Adirondacks, Troy was actually one of the richest cities in the union. My house is directly across the street from the Burden Iron Works. Henry Burden. He had a high production factory in the 1800s that could make a horseshoe a second. Imagine that.

They say, though, in the 1980s, like during the crack epidemic, people were afraid to even come downtown. But in my years here, there's been a real revitalization. Part of the "Main Street America" movement. Today, downtown has this buzzy, artistic, vibe. Mom-and-pop shops. An amazing farmer's market. In fact, last year, the Troy Riverfront Farmer's Market won Best Farmer's Market *in the fucking nation*. For quite a while now, too, we've been located in the heart of the farmer's market.

For some reason, I refer to the company as a "we." When I say "we," it's really just me. Although we do sell work by local artists. And Rosemarie is set up inside the store now, too. It's one of the smartest decisions we've ever made. Earlier this year, we built her a little salon in the back of Weathered Wood where she specializes in cuts for queer clients. And also does her energy work, you know, physical and emotional healing.

So COVID definitely put a damper on things for both of us. But Rosemarie has been back to work a lot. People need their hair cut! And the store is open for business as well. Right after my accident, the community rallied, contributed to a GoFundMe, and helped me buy a new van. Sales are way down, yeah, but there are still people who want me to build them some custom stuff. For now, we'll just accomplish what we can accomplish. Keep the lights on. Survive.

*

On May 25th, the police murdered Mr. George Floyd. For more than eight minutes, they had a knee on his neck while onlookers videotaped. I was fucking outraged. How could you not be? That Saturday, we went to an afternoon rally in Albany, and it was powerful to see so many people standing up, speaking out, and saying, "No. We're not going to tolerate this anymore!" That night, in Albany, there were riots.

We held a couple of our own peaceful demonstrations in front of the police station here in Troy. Me, Rosemarie, and a handful of other people. We're not like civil rights leaders, though, so we had no idea what we were doing. But we *showed up*, you know, engaged officers as they entered and exited the building. Put them on the spot. They'd say things like: "We hear you." And: "We're doing a lot to change." Bullshit. We all know it. Like Rage Against the Machine says, "Some of those that work forces / are the same that burn crosses."

When word came down that there was going to be a big Black Lives Matter rally in downtown Troy, we were really excited. One day, though, like a week before the rally, we saw the storeowner across the street walk out with all of this plywood. He started boarding up his windows. And then we heard news from the other side of downtown: a bunch of restaurants had also boarded up. The next thing you know, the entire fucking downtown had boarded up. That mentality, that fear, took off like wildfire.

I didn't want to board up, but it's not my property. The landlord said to me: "Well, Danny, if those 15-foot tall windows get smashed, *those windows that cost $5,000 apiece*, then it's on you to replace them." We're still in the middle of this crazy pandemic, remember, and right as New York State was allowing retail stores and restaurants to begin re-opening. And now, our entire downtown looked like a war zone! I was furious. Because that shit sends the wrong message. That we're more concerned about property damage than we are about the atrocities going on in this country.

The first night that the boards went up, crowds of people came out and plastered the town with inspiring messages about the movement. I put up a BLACK LIVES MATTER sign. And another that said BLACK-OWNED BUSINESS. Local graffiti artists and painters went around and used the boards as canvases. Some of the business owners blared music into the street. It was like a block party, a little creative festival, you know what I mean? There was so much positive energy.

The next morning, however, I was heartbroken. In the middle of the night, some slimy lowlifes had spray-painted across my storefront: ALL LIVES MATTER.

Lately, I only wear Black Lives Matter gear when I leave the house. So, you know, I get into a lot of "conversations" with these All Lives Matter people. Like two days ago, I ran into a local guy. Some friend of a friend. He saw me pull up, and as soon as I got out of my van, he said, "Oh, no, Danny, all lives matter, *all* lives matter." Okay. It depends on my mood whether or not I want to entertain these assholes. I explained, "Yes, all lives do matter. *However*, disproportionately, black people are killed by cops. Black lives are in danger *right now*."

That's the simplest way to answer the All Lives Matter people. It's either that, you know, or give them a superman punch right to their fucking face. But I'm not trying to go back to jail anytime soon, so...

*

In the days before the rally, we put everything on hold and threw ourselves wholeheartedly into the movement. We decided to turn Weathered Wood into "protest central." We put out calls on social media for volunteers and donations, and the community responded. Masks, snacks, and bottled water came piling into the store. People gathered out front to make homemade signs.

The morning of the actual protest, I passed out snacks and water, but spent 90% of my day patrolling the crowd, looking for bad actors. One kid came into the store early to drop off a donation. He wasn't with anybody. And his entire face was covered. Like fully-wrapped. Protestors were wearing face coverings, but this felt *odd* to me. We had everyone who donated sign a registry, so we could send thank-you notes. But when I asked, "Do you want to sign the registry?" He said, "Nope." And just walked away. *Way* away.

So I followed him for a little bit with a couple of my friends. A loosely-assembled security team. He stood in a section where you couldn't even hear the speakers. With his arms crossed. Not clapping. We kept an eye on him. Took a couple of pictures. And then went and asked the police: "Is there any chance someone can have a talk with this kid? Find out his story." And the police said, "No way. We're not going into that crowd."

Fucking great. All over the country, there have been counter-protestors at rallies looking to incite violence. Some of these crazies, you know, have been running protestors over with their cars. This kid could have had a knife? Or a gun? Like the kid who shot up that church, Dylann Roof, he sat down and prayed with the people he eventually massacred. And that was a small group. We had 11,000 people in Troy that day. I thought, "Holy shit! There could be dangerous players anywhere."

That was *before* we even encountered the scary dudes at the Uncle Sam bus stop. Wearing flak jackets. Carrying knives and billy clubs! I yelled out, "What the hell are you doing here?" And they said, "We're here to defend *your* first amendment rights." Yeah right. So we pushed our way through the crowd, up to the stage, and gathered the biggest brothers we could find. By the time the flak jacket guys were approaching the crowd, we had like 200 people there to confront them, *surround* them, and say, collectively: "You're not welcome here. We want you to go."

The police *claimed*, after the fact, you know, that they had eyes on these guys the whole time. And maybe you heard about this on the news? In their cars, police found loaded guns without serial numbers. Gas masks. And a tactical militia manual. One of these guys was active military! They were from an organization called The New England Minutemen. Affiliated with the Boogaloo Boys. Insane rightwing dudes who think white men are being marginalized in our society. They're looking to start a second Civil War.

So that's what was going on in *our* city. Fucking psychopaths with firearms. Two blocks from my store. I told that story over and over and over, so many times, until Rosemarie got sick of hearing about it. She was like, "Bro, it was a community protest, not the fucking 'Danny Show.'" But you know how it is. Danny loves the limelight!

*

In a few days, at some city building behind the DMV in Troy, county legislators are meeting. To fundraise for the mayor. And congratulate each other on what a great job they did at the rally. So there's a group here in town – Justice for Dahmeek – planning a vigil-style protest outside. To let the city know that we are unhappy with this response.

Dahmeek McDonald. An unarmed Black man. Shot in the arm by police. One bullet even grazed his head. Dahmeek survived, but that cop was never charged. This has been happening in Troy, over and over, for years. In 2016, the police *murdered* an unarmed Black man, Edson Thevenin. And the city, right up to the mayor, they covered it up. And the cop that murdered Edson Thevenin, he actually just died of COVID. So they'll be honoring him specifically at this event. Why are you honoring him? He was just a part of the systemic racist policing that goes on in this fucking country. Why are we publicly celebrating him?

Never mind the budget that Troy just passed. I can get you a copy. For 2020, they allotted $207,000 for Public Health. And guess how much they gave to the police? Twenty million dollars! Twenty *million*. It's atrocious. We have a tiny little city, and our police have a fucking tank. I'm not kidding. They have a vehicle in their arsenal that can withstand an RPG. What do they need with that? Why aren't they figuring how to commit some of that money to poor communities and better treatment of minorities?

Everything is so fucked up. For a while now, the only thing that I've wanted to do is make art. I can't sit still. Or hang out or read or even watch TV. I just need some release. So, at night, I've been going in my backyard, having a couple of cocktails, and painting by the fire. I gesso a bunch of boards, hang them on my fence, and then layer them with color. A combination of acrylics and spray paint in wild swirly motions. My art teacher from prison, we're still in touch, and when he saw the work, he described it as *energetic*.

More recently, I've been painting outside of the shop. Thursday, Friday, and Saturday nights, they shut down the block and let restaurants put their tables in the street. And I'm down there anyways, you know, so I put on little performances. Last Friday, I whipped out a painting in 45 minutes. And then poured on some chainsaw gas. Lit part of it on fire. Somebody posted a crazy picture of me on Instagram. Barefoot and shirtless. Ripped jean shorts. Gray beard. Bald. I'm always surprised when I see myself in pictures. How *big* I am. It's like, "Geez. I look like fucking sasquatch."

So I'm building some hype for the work, yeah, and I have sold a few pieces already. But these paintings are really supposed to be a cathartic kind of thing. To get away from all of the overwhelming seriousness. And just be immersed in the movements of the universe itself. Tap into some place that's free from the day-to-day anxieties of being a fucking human on Earth. It's not so much what I'm trying to express, but more where I'm trying to get mentally. Or what I'm trying to get past.

Because the righteous indignation that I feel. It's almost a block for me to be able to live my life. Between my own history with the system. And this ongoing and unresolved situation with the local police. Everything's been slow, you know, so I don't even have a court date until August. And then to see all of these Black people being killed in the streets. And then, throughout the pandemic, the general lack of leadership in this country. The disregard for human life is fucking horrifying.

It's almost enough to make me want to go back to robbing banks.

STAIRWAY TO HEAVEN

1970-1991

Oklahoma City, Oklahoma. That's where I was born. December 18th, in the year of our Lord, 1970. My parents were college students. Father: Black. Mother: Ukrainian. They were young and not very interested in being parents. I don't know much. Just what I've been told. The first day of my life most likely involved me being taken from my mother. And sent off to the orphanage.

For six months or so, the people at the orphanage called me Richard. Until I was adopted by a couple of crazy Christian evangelists, and they changed my name to Daniel. Like the dude who was thrown to the lions. My adoptive parents: Robert and Sandra Killion. Who knows how they found me? They were living in New Hampshire at the time, but moved around a lot when I was a kid. All over New England. From New Hampshire, to Maine for a while, and then Connecticut, where they settled down, finally, in the shitty little town of Wolcott.

I say "crazy Christian evangelists." In my personal opinion, Christian evangelists are all fucking crazy. What denomination were they? I don't know. Evangelical! Like the Falwells. Jim and Tammy Faye Bakker. The PTL Club. "Prosperity Theology." Your Christian faith and charity will be rewarded *financially*. Jim and Tammy Faye Bakker, though, they ended up being scam artists who would *cry cry cry* on television: "Oh! The poor children!" Meanwhile, they were buying Mercedes after Mercedes. Had an air-conditioned dog house in the yard.

As for Robert and Sandra, they made it their mission in life to adopt special needs children. I was their first.

Numero uno. One of nine. My special need was... being Black? If you can believe that shit. My brother Mike was next. Michael Gabriel. Another Biblical name. In Maine, my parents belonged to a church, and their pastor's daughter got knocked up by a Hells Angel. I was five years old when they adopted Mike, and then he bounced around with us the whole time.

And then came Elizabeth. She had Fetal Alcohol Syndrome. And Laura: completely mentally challenged, IQ in the 40s, schizophrenia, significant emotional problems. Christy and Julie: both from Korea. They came over as sisters, but I don't think they're actually related. Christy was 100% blind. Julie was *legally* blind, but can read something if she puts her face up close. And then Minnie: also from Korea. And Anna: from an orphanage in Haiti. Lastly: Kevin. Severe, severe, issues. No language skills. Didn't speak at all.

That's everybody. Well, Robert and Sandra also had a daughter of their own, Sheri, older than me. She was actually the first. So: Sheri, Danny, Mike, Elizabeth, Christy, Julie, Minnie, Anna, Kevin... who am I missing? Sheri, Danny, Mike, Elizabeth, Christy, Julie, Anna, Kevin... Laura! Wow. I'm still missing someone. Right now, I'm wondering, have I been counting wrong all of these years?

*

One of my earliest memories. Seeing a lobster. I was maybe five years old, living in Maine, and swimming in the ocean. Alone. Underwater. With my eyes open. I've always loved to swim. As far as I can remember, I've just always known how. I really don't recall anybody ever teaching me.

Certainly not Robert and Sandra. They had ten children, but I don't think they were good parents to any of them. Their whole mission was to impress the church. That's my theory. They were just trying to get cool with

Jesus. When it came to actually caring for their kids, they did a fucking terrible job! Put a roof over our heads. Gave us food to eat. Okay, but didn't ever really *love* us, you know what I mean? I never received any of the affection that children need for their well-being.

The thing that drives me crazy: people kept giving them children! Every time God spoke to Sandra, I ended up with another sibling. That's how they determined who to adopt. It's ridiculous. Obviously. And God's communication skills were imperfect, you know, or Sandra's hearing was off. Because, at one point, God told her that they would be getting a deaf child. So we were all instructed to learn sign language. Instead of a deaf child, though, we ended up with Christy and Julie. The two blind girls from Korea. A lot of fucking good sign language would've done us!

Looking back, Sandra must have been driving the operation. Robert just worked a ton. And bitched a lot. When you took on a child, some of the states would give you a monthly subsidy until the kid turned 18. They probably depended on that money. Sandra had to stay home and look after everything. And he worked at a food distribution warehouse for this big Connecticut grocery store chain called IGA, you know, loading food onto trucks. So I have no idea how great of a Christian he was. I always thought he was a fucking authoritarian piece of shit.

Here's a memory. Robert liked to fish and sometimes would invite me and my brother Mike to come along. After a kid from the neighborhood had shot out one of his car windows with a BB-gun, Robert replaced the window with a piece of plexiglass. This was probably August when we piled into the car to go fishing. It was like 100 degrees in the car, you know, and I forgot about the plexiglass. So when I rolled down the window, the plexiglass slipped out of place. And Robert yelled, "You fucking asshole!" Punched me right in the stomach.

I was a little closer with Sandra. The mother figure. She was more fun. At Thanksgiving, I remember, she would make the turkey stand up and dance on its dead little turkey legs. One time, we were all watching TV in the living room. And they wanted me to stop talking. Sandra had a cup of hot cocoa. It wasn't *that* hot, you know, but she said, "If you don't shut up, I'm going to pour this cocoa on your head." So I dared her. And... she did it. Poured the cocoa right on my head. Everybody laughing. Haha.

I don't want you to think that there was a lot of physical abuse. For the most part, it was *measured*. So if Robert was at work, and I'd have an argument with Sandra, raise my voice to her, you know, then I would get sent to my room. One afternoon, I remember, he came home, and she told him: "You need to deal with Danny." So he stormed into my room and found me hiding by the side of the bed. He didn't even try to sit down and talk to me. Nah. He just started hitting. But, again, I never got a broken bone. Never any serious bruises. It was *measured*.

And not that it stopped me from doing whatever I wanted. By the time I was 11, 12, 13 years old, I was staying out late. Drinking and smoking weed with my friends. If I was out *too* late, they would lock me out of the house. I spent multiple winter nights shivering out in the cold. I wouldn't want to wake anyone up, so I'd go sleep in Robert's van. One morning, he drove all the way to work. The next town over. And I just laid quietly in the back of the van, waited until he was inside the warehouse, and then walked home.

Early in my childhood, there was some ceremonial punishment. They'd spank us with an old table leg. At some point, however, they said, "We want you to behave, but we're not going to hit you anymore." And then made this big fucking ordeal of burning the spanking stick in the fireplace. After that, when I'd misbehave, there would be wailing. And gnashing of teeth. Robert would bring me into the bedroom, open up the Bible, and point to the verse: "Honor thy mother and father." And I'd be like, "Yeah, but you're not my mother and father. Why should I care?"

It's funny. In retrospect, even as a kid, always, *always*, I remember thinking, "What the fuck is this nonsense? These people. They're so full of shit."

*

At a certain age, I stopped going to church with my family. I just decided, you know, that was it for me. When Sandra yelled for everyone to get dressed and ready for church, I went outside: "Alright. I'll be in the car!" And then took off down the street.

Church wasn't really in a church. Sandra's sister and her husband also fostered children. And Sandra's sister's *daughter* also adopted children. And then she married a guy, this pastor named Bob Cronk. They had some of their own children, but then fostered and adopted more. And we all went to "church" in their suburban living room. What was that like? Fucking *weird*. It still creeps me out to think about it. My extended family, you know, and a few other people. They'd have their hands in the air. Jumping up and down. "Praise Jesus! Praise Jesus!" Singing and dancing around. Possessed by the spirit.

Bob Cronk. The pastor. He was a total dick! You know those patriarchal Christian men, who stand in the pulpit and preach the sermon, but then in their own lives, they're like not nice people. Abrasive and unpleasant. Yelled a lot. Mean to his kids. I remember his oldest son would sit there, 15 years old, you know, just sucking on his two fingers. And Bob Cronk would get all mad. And when Bob Cronk got mad, he looked up to the sky. His eyes rolling back into his cranium.

I look back at the men in that community. How fucking shitty they were. Robert and Sandra, of course, were always trying to get me out of their hair. So they would drop me off at my aunt and uncle's house. Once, I was over there, you know, in the driveway. Picking up rocks and tossing them toward this little pond. My uncle, I guess, had told me to stop throwing rocks, but I didn't stop. So he fucking smacked me in the face. Really hard. All of those people, man, they were so unloving. Emotionally unstable.

At 12 years old, I was pretty tall. Almost six feet already. And there was a woman, you know, a member of the church. She'd be in this room. Front row. Singing and dancing. Praising Jesus. She had two younger boys, so after the service, we went into the yard, and I threw the football around with her kids. She asked my parents: "Hey, do you think Danny might want to come hang out with my boys? Maybe go to the aquarium." So we went to the Mystic Aquarium. She parked. And then said to her kids: "Get out of the car!" We smoked weed, right there in the parking lot, before going inside.

Another time, Robert and Sandra shipped me over to this same woman's house for a sleepover. So I was there, and she was cooking dinner. Her husband and his friend came home. They're hanging out. Drinking beers. And then they got ready to go for a ride. And she suggested, "Oh, why don't you take Danny along?" So they did. And took me to a bar. Where they bought a fucking eight ball of cocaine! And then brought me back to the house. They said, "We're heading back to the bar for the night. You can't come, but here. Take some of this." They left *me* some of the cocaine! Put it in the freezer, you know, to enjoy at my leisure.

So this woman put her kids to bed, and I sat there on the couch, by myself, fucking *geeked* out of my mind on cocaine! And that was my first experience. With cocaine.

*

Between the ages of 10 and 18, some of it's kind of muddy. Hard to differentiate, you know, exactly when I was what age. Part of it might be the drugs and alcohol. But I also was moved around a lot. Sometimes I lived in Robert and Sandra's house. Sometimes in drug rehab. Sometimes in juvenile detention. Yeah, from the time that we moved to Wolcott, starting in 5th grade, from that point on, I was always in some kind of trouble.

Upon arriving in Connecticut, we first lived in Waterbury. Your typical post-industrial city. Half an hour southwest of Hartford. And Wolcott is just a crappy little white suburb outside of Waterbury. Not super rich, but not slummy, either. A town, you know, like any other. Connecticut's only the third biggest state in the union, but it has *so many* towns. I swear, you can take a casual afternoon walk and pass through three different towns like Wolcott.

School was okay. I liked being around other kids. Meeting people. And I was well-liked. Had a lot of girlfriends. But I was *hyper*. Didn't listen well. Couldn't pay attention. Couldn't sit still. Like I was supposed to be learning to the play the saxophone, but never practiced. So I'd ride my saxophone case around the hallways. I remember, clearly, some teacher yelling at me for some shit. And I just looked at him and said, "Fuck you! I don't have to do what you say." And then walked out of class, out of the school entirely, and into the woods.

I wasn't dumb. I liked science. History a little bit. Drawing. Being creative. I feel like I could have learned better if they had been willing to find better ways to teach me. I wasn't a good speller. Didn't like English. The English language is so fucking retarded. Ph is "f" and f is "f." C'mon! Eventually, they said I was "learning disabled." That was the label they attached to me. It was so devastating to my self-esteem, you know, that by the time I was in high school, I had completely checked out. Didn't give a fuck. Took mescaline in the mornings. Would regularly go to school wasted.

They put me in a class with only like four other kids. The "special class," you know what I mean? I just sat there and drew in my notebook. Skulls and shit. Satanic-looking doodles. The Metallica logo. I remember, being at my desk, not paying attention, drawing, and the teacher – who was super fucking hot! – she yelled, "Danny!" And I looked up: "What?" She walked over and peeked at my notebook. Whatever she saw, it must have been pretty disturbing. Because she said, "I'm taking this to the principal's office." I got all upset, grabbed the notebook back from her, and ran out of the classroom.

And then there was some meeting. With me, Robert and Sandra, and an assigned school counselor. I told them: "You adopted me and you're my parents. I really want to be involved with sports." I still have so much resentment about this. I remember, driving through Wolcott for the first time and seeing Pop Warner in the neighborhood. And wanting to play so badly. Football. Baseball. Basketball. Every sport! That's *all* I wanted to do. But Robert said to the counselor: "Huh. I never play sports with Danny in the yard. Because he doesn't have very good hand-eye coordination."

After the counseling, I somehow ended up on a baseball team. The Athletics. Robert showed up to *one* fucking game. Didn't go into the bleachers. Didn't sit down or cheer or anything. Just stood in the parking lot with his arms crossed, you know, like, "Here I am." So I only played baseball for that one season. There was a total lack of family support for my interest in sports. And I also didn't really get along with any of my teammates. I ended up falling into a crowd that wasn't into sports. Instead, my friends were into getting drunk, smoking weed, and taking drugs.

I mean, thinking back, for the most part, I was still a happy-go-lucky kid. Rebellious at a young age, yeah, but like… upbeat. I'd goof around and laugh and be silly. I have this weird eyeball tattoo on my bicep, you know, but underneath, there's actually a tattoo of a smiley face. That was my first tattoo. I did it myself. When I was in my first drug rehab. Using a technique called "stick and poke." You take a sewing needle. Wrap thread around it. Dip it in the

India ink and then poke a hole in your skin. And that's how you make your image. One dot at a time.

*

Even as a kid, I was my own person. I just did me, you know what I mean? As much as possible, I tried to not be around the Killion family. Preferred to be out and about. Hanging with my friends. Having fun.

My closest friend growing up was named Tom Diesel. His dad was a vicious, vicious, alcoholic. A-medium-sized-bottle-of-Calvert-whiskey-every-morning-to-stop-the-shakes alcoholic. Mechanic. Owned his own garage. But we would do work around the yard sometimes, and he would pay us with a case of beer! And then just let us hang out and drink. The five of us. Me, Tom, Eric Shiffaletti, and Mike and Sean Flaherty. Tom's dad kept some old cars in the backyard, you know, the ones where the backseats face each other. Those John Dillinger/Tommy gun cars. So we would sit in them. Drink. Smoke pot. And try to finger chicks.

We had a bicycle chop shop back there, too! We'd steal bikes and store them in this big garage. That's how we tore around the neighborhood, you know, as a little clique. And, if something broke, if we needed any part, a rim, a petal, whatever, then we'd just go in the garage. My bike, I remember, had chopper forks. And I cut up a whole bunch of Budweiser cans and attached them all around. I called it the Budmobile. Not even old enough to drive and already obsessed with Budweiser!

We would build these cool tree forts, you know, climb way up in a tree, nail a bunch of boards in place, and make a platform. Sit up there and drink beer. And the Flaherty brothers lived close to a lake. They had a boat with one of those tiny little motors. And there was this big rock that jutted up from the middle of the lake. So we'd take the boat out there and drink on the rock. Their family's house also had this sweet basement. Brady Bunch-style, '70s decor, with a pool table. And *a bar*.

Once, we found a ton of Black Beauties in their parents' dresser drawer. So we ate all of that speed and then walked 12 miles to the roller skating rink. Roller Magic in Waterbury. That was the place, man! We had our own breakdancing group called the Systematic Breakers and danced in competitions at the Roller Magic. Take turns, you know, doing our little routines. Eric would do a bunch of moves and then run towards me. And I'd lock my fingers together and flip him backwards. He'd do this amazing flip, *fly through the air*, land, and then keep on breakdancing. True fucking story.

We also shoplifted like crazy. Fuck yeah. All of the time. Jolly Ranchers and whole cartons of cigarettes from Cumberland Farms. Like back in the day when cigarettes weren't stored behind the counter. We'd shove everything into our Bomber jackets. Those winter coats with lots of pockets. One time, leaving a K-Mart, we ran over to Toys "R" Us, one parking lot over, and started pulling the booty out of our coats. But the security guards from K-Mart were having lunch in that parking lot. So they saw us, you know, and dragged us back to the office. Busted!

I was never scared of cops. I remember, there was this water tower, and we would climb the ladder to the top. You could see everything up there, you know, looking out over the towns of Connecticut. One night, the cops showed up and tried to clear us out. There were probably 15-20 kids. Partying. And the cops were yelling at us to come down. Everyone else did, but not me. Nope. I was like, "I'm staying the fuck up here." I thought that if I waited long enough, the cops would just leave.

So... they had to come up and get me. I remember, being in the back of the police car. In handcuffs. Slightly drunk, you know, routing through the backseat. Fiddling with shit. I somehow found the mace, touched it, and even set it off a little bit. The officer was so pissed! When we got to the station, he locked me in a cell, and was like, "Oh, you want to play with mace, asshole?" And then reached through the bars. And sprayed me straight in the face!

Fucking cops.

*

My first *real* trouble with the law started this way.

We had heard about a house party in town. Some stupid parents had gone on vacation and let their daughter stay home. You know how it goes. She invited over all of her friends. A group of kids that we didn't really hang with. The jock set. But then, of course, a ton of people showed up to this party. When we arrived, late, everyone was drunk off their asses. And the house was fucking pummeled. Like completely destroyed. This place was destroyed *when we got there*.

I'm not claiming to be innocent. We thought it was hilarious that everything was all smashed up. And, yeah, yeah, we might have smashed some stuff, too. No doubt. I participated on some level. But me and like two other dudes were blamed for the whole thing! No one else at that party, you know, got into any fucking trouble. They were the athletes, and we were the potheads. The "bad" kids.

As a minor, they gave me some kind of probation, but then I didn't follow up. Missed some court dates. So they sent me to a detention center in New Haven. Juvenile detention, you know, juvie. It's jail *for kids*. I just remember flashes of what it looked like. How it felt. Cold and metal and gray. The cell blocks were designed to be easily controlled from something called a "bubble." This office in the middle where COs could see down the various hallways, you know, the rows of cells housing teenagers.

I made a couple of friends. Me and my cellmate, I remember, would get excited to rent a radio for the night. There was one kid who was like a super hustler, you know, had a little store in his cell. Where he sold chips and honey buns. Whatever. And we'd rent a radio from him. Listen to the overnight deejay on WHCC, the local radio station out of Hartford, where Howard Stern got his start. Other than that... I don't know. It was hard, but I got by. Went out in the yard. Played cards. Called home and cried.

I only stayed in detention for a few months. Until my case was sorted out. Nothing happens overnight. There are court appearances and meetings. They eventually let me out of juvie and sent me to a drug rehab center. Court-mandated. For 18 months. A place called DayTop, this state-funded program for heroin addicts, but they had an offshoot, specifically for minors, called Alpha House. It was in a historical brick building. We all intermingled during the day. Ate meals together and shit. And then the junkies slept on one half of the house, and the kids slept on the other.

There would be these group meetings, you know, like big family gatherings. And whenever someone got off probation, they had to stand up in front of the whole community and sing a song. This was called "Giving It Away." I remember some old dopeheads absolutely killing "In the Still of the Night" barbershop-style. My first time, I sang "Stairway to Heaven." It went very, very, *very* badly. Haha. After getting in trouble, though, and going back on, and then back off probation for a second time, I sang "War Pigs" by Black Sabbath. And got a standing ovation!

Fooling around in the house was strictly forbidden. But what were they thinking? A bunch of teenagers living together! Wild times. A few months in, me, this girl who had a crush on me, another girl *who I had a crush on*, and her boyfriend, we all decided to split. We walked to the bus station. Bought tickets to Newport, Rhode Island. Went to Newport. Swam in the ocean. Slept on the beach for a couple of nights. And then got jobs at restaurants. Even rented our own fucking apartment!

Yeah, man, we lived in that apartment for a while, worked restaurant jobs, and hung out on the beach, you know, on the run from rehab. That was fun.

*

I was 17 years old by the time that situation was somewhat resolved. And then living back in Robert and Sandra's house again, but still on probation. I was pretty concerned. Questioning myself. This road wasn't leading me anywhere. I knew that I needed to be better if I wanted to survive in this world.

There was no going back to high school, so I started working as a mechanic at a Meineke Car Care Center. I didn't really have any mechanical skills, no, but changing exhaust systems isn't that hard, you know what I mean? So I did that for a while and then became really depressed. Began drugging and drinking a lot again. The manager at this Meineke was a big partier, and we would party so fucking hard. On the weekends, you know, doing tons and tons of cocaine.

I got fired from that job. Because I was partying on a Friday night, the day we got paid, but then had to work on Saturday morning. I didn't make it in. And... I got fired. And I knew that this would put me in huge trouble with probation. One of my sisters, you know, was on some really powerful tranquilizers. So... I swallowed the whole bottle. Like I was just ready to be dead. Sandra was yelling, "C'mon, Danny! You have to get to work!" But I had already taken this whole bottle of tranquilizers and gone back to bed.

I woke up, three days later. In a straight jacket! In a rubber room! No joke. It even had that door with the tiny window, you know what I mean? And the doctor, this psychiatrist, I could see his little eyeball peeking through. I'll never forget. When the doctor walked in, the first thing that he said. He told me that my face was *asymmetrical*. And I remember thinking, "Wow. That's a pretty rude thing to say to a patient. What the fuck is wrong with you?" Haha.

This psychiatric hospital – The Institute of Living – was on a big compound in Hartford, and I stayed there for 11 months. It was pretty bizarre. Because I just had depression, you know, but I wasn't like crazy. And there were some *legit* crazy people at this place. Schizophrenics. On heavy doses of medication. Some adults, but mostly teenagers. One kid, I remember, he would never open his eyes. The only thing he cared about was smoking cigarettes, you know, so he'd stand by the door all day, fidgeting furiously, waiting to go outside.

They separated boys from the girls in the dorm. And I remember getting caught on the girls' side. Multiple times. With Diane Simmons. She knew I liked rock music, and I was listening to a lot of Metallica, so she gave me an Anthrax cassette. Diane wore a lot of makeup, had really big hair, and was *very much* from New Jersey. And... she wanted to make out with me. So I was in her room, and some staff member was banging on the door: "Danny, come on out! We know you're in there!" Busted!

For the most part, I had fun there. Didn't have a lot of responsibility. It was an easy way to live. You had your own room. You'd wake up. Go to a counseling session. Spend the rest of your day hanging out. Listening to music. Playing foosball. I remember throwing the football around with some guy who worked there. And jumping over the foosball table to make a catch. And the ball hit the tip of my pinkie. Dislocated it sideways. Ever since then, you know, my pinkie is crooked. From that time I tried to catch a football over a foosball table in the psych ward.

After I was released from the psychiatric hospital, they put me in a halfway house in Hartford and made me get a job. So I worked, briefly, at McDonald's. How was that? What do you think? It fucking sucked! Flipping burgers. Wearing that stupid hat. Saying: "Welcome to McDonald's. May I take your order, please?" I don't know how people work there. Those kinds of chains, you know, if you're not doing something every second that you're on the clock, then they try to make you feel bad about it. "If you've got time to lean, you've got time to clean." That's what they say.

To get to and from work, I had to take the bus. But there was a girl at the halfway house who let me borrow her bike. So I started riding this girl's bike to work. At McDonald's. In the wintertime. I remember, riding home, at night, after working a whole shift. I rode over some railroad tracks and wiped out real hard in the snow. Hopped back on the bike, you know, and headed home to the halfway house. My probation officer just happened to pull up next to me. He was like, "Danny! What are you doing? You haven't checked in with probation in weeks!"

*

Back in the world, I didn't go home to Wolcott. No. I moved to New Britain, Connecticut. Got my own apartment. And a job at a restaurant called Chuck's Steakhouse. I started as a dishwasher, but worked my way up to prep cook, and eventually, to the grill.

Restaurants are super ripe. If you even have a hint of a substance abuse problem, and you start working in a restaurant, then you're going to be in deep shit. Put it this way. At Chuck's, we sometimes watched the sun come up in the bar. They actually ended up taking the place away from the first owner. Because he would run off to Key West, blow all of his money on coke, and the payroll checks would bounce. So, yeah, it was a fucking party restaurant. That's how we got down!

On busy nights, the manager, Cliff, would come around and ask the grill cooks if we needed anything. And then he'd bring us shots of JD! There were also shift drinks: a free drink at the end of every shift. I'd sit right at the bar, you know, underage. Every now and then, Cliff would kick me out. But, mostly, he didn't care. I remember turning 20 years old at the restaurant, but telling everybody that I was turning 21. All night, people showered me with booze.

I've always been a hard worker, though. My first gig, going way back, 12 years old, was at a gun club in Wolcott. You would go down into this little half underground concrete shed where there were boxes of clay pigeons. These bright orange circles of clay. The shooter yells, "Pull!" And someone outside pushes a button. And then, inside the shed, this big fucking menacing mechanical arm whips around: "Fwooooom!" And you drop in the pigeon. And then rip your hand away as fast as possible. Like it wasn't automated. There was actually some kid, hidden away, loading the machine.

That kid was me! I would get paid like 75 cents per shot. And the little pits were always flooded. And there were rats down there. So you're a kid, you know, trudging through floodwater, beating back rats with a broom. There was another employee at the club who would talk mad shit to me. Like racist shit. Right to my face. He would say like, "Go back in that shack, boy! Before I get my shackles!" This kid was way older than me, and I was so young. I didn't understand what the hell he was talking about.

As a teenager, I also worked with my Uncle Mike. Dude wasn't really my uncle. He was like the foster son of Sandra's sister. Whatever that makes him to me! But I worked with him as like a general laborer. Chopping firewood. Shoveling snow off of roofs. A lot of tree work. One time, he was up in a tree with a chainsaw, and dropped it, and the chainsaw caught his shirt, and went "Rrrrrrrrrr!" Right up his neck. I was like, "Holy shit!" But this motherfucker. The next day, he was back at work with a still fresh chainsaw wound across his face.

Later on, too, I worked for a tree service. Driving around in those big ass trucks, you know, the ones with the booms. There was a crew of us on every truck. One guy would cut away branches from power lines. While the rest of us put the fallen branches through a wood chipper.

I got fired from that job. Because we all had to go to some safety meeting at the power company. After the meeting, my foreman was like, "We're not going back to work today, fellas. We're going to the strip club!" So we went to a strip club. And never went back to work. The next day, the whole crew was fired.

That's the only job I ever got fired from. Well, no, there was the Meineke. And I also got fired from Chuck's Steakhouse. Me and another kid. We were stealing money from the office. There were these buckets where they pooled the tips, and we'd sneak a couple of $20s out of each envelope. Until we got *busted*. But then, six months later, I went back there and apologized. Begged for my job back. And for some reason – who knows why? – they fucking gave it to me.

*

It was at Chuck's that I met Erica. She was a hostess there, and I tried to get her to date me, but she heard that I had slept with one of the waitresses. So she was like, "No way. You're a dog!" And I might have been. Before I met her.

Erica was my first serious girlfriend. How did I win her over? Persistence, I guess. And I also knew that she liked trucks. So when my car died, I bought an old pickup truck. She had long curly dirty-blonde hair. Pretty blue eyes. Wore cowboy boots. And loved to ride around in my truck with the radio blasting: "So caught up in you, little girl!" You know that song by 38 Special? She'd be dancing in the front seat. Her hair flying everywhere. And when she was drunk, she would lay her head down in my lap. And I thought she… was… awesome.

Erica was born in Connecticut, but had spent most of her childhood in California. After we met, her family moved back to California, but she stayed in Connecticut, and moved in with me. Yeah, it was like a regular domestic relationship. We lived together, worked together, ate together. Although she never introduced me to her family. It turns out: her dad was super racist. We came home one day to a nasty message on our answering machine. He was screaming, "Erica, I heard you're living with some fucking n***** c**n! This better not be true!"

We stayed together for a while after that, but then, you know, it kind of dwindled. I was drinking a lot. Behaving immaturely. Not being a very good partner. Initially, I broke up with her. And then went running back: "I made a mistake. Let's try to make it work!" But then she was like, "No. No. No. It's done." This *potentially* had something to do with my pursuit of other women. I don't know, man. She just wanted me to grow up. Act like an adult. I was like, "What? I'm only 21!"

Heartbroken, I decided that I'd show her. So I joined the military. I actually wanted to be a Marine. But when I went to the recruiter's office, the Marine guy was out to lunch. The Navy guy was there, though, so... I joined the Navy. Because of my criminal record, they said they'd have to pull some strings. C'mon! If you're willing to be brainwashed into their system, you know, and if you're willing to get killed over some bullshit, they don't give a fuck abut your past.

I went to boot camp in Chicago. The Great Mistakes. Super cliché. Picture boot camp in the movies. It was exactly like that. We got off of the bus, and everyone was so friendly. They gave us a tour. We turned in our street clothes for military uniforms. And then, you know, at 11:00 on that first night, we settled into bed. But then, at 4:00 in the morning, they came rushing in. Banging on trash can lids. Screaming and yelling: "Get up, maggots! Get up, scum! Get your ass in line!"

The military really harps on you being able to function on a minimum amount of sleep. Like you're some sort of pussy if you sleep more than four hours in a night. And when we got in trouble, they'd make us stand at attention. Next to our bunks. For hours at a time. Once, on hardly any sleep, I leaned against my bunk when we were supposed to be standing at attention. And fell asleep. Standing on my feet. And then collapsed. Didn't even realize I was asleep, you know, until I hit the ground.

But I liked boot camp. On Day 1, the guy who led our troop, he came up to me: "You! You're a big guy. I'm making you Master-at-Arms. You're in charge of everybody in the barracks." I just looked tough, I guess, so he put me in charge. Of when to get up, when to shower, when to march. I was like, "Alright. Cool." Some of these other dudes, you know, were there to get engineering or computer jobs. They were pretty out of shape! So, on runs, I would run from the back of the pack, all the way to the front, and then circle everyone again. Taunting them as I ran by.

I excelled in the structure of boot camp. After that, however, I got stationed at the sub base in Groton, Connecticut. And never really became very close with anyone there. Was lonely and depressed. Only a few weeks on the base, I went to my superiors and told them: "I hate this. I'm miserable. I'm going to kill myself." So they hauled me off to a psych ward and loaded me up with Prozac. And then, just like that, I was medically discharged from the Navy. My military career was over.

I found myself back with Robert and Sandra. Again. Living in this little pool house in their backyard. I was still trying to fix things with Erica. I remember, she actually stayed over with me for a night. In the pool house. But I could tell, she thought, "This guy is totally off his rocker." So we broke up for good. And that. Was the end. Of that.

*

When you wash out of the Navy, and you're a high school dropout, it's impossible not to think, "Holy shit! Where the fuck is my life going?"

Well, I did drop out of high school. But *technically…* I graduated. Me and two other friends went to a night school program at the Waterbury town hall. Clearly, we weren't crushing night school either, so one of the teachers took pity on us. She was like, "Listen. Here are the answers that you'll you need to pass the final test. I can't stand to have kids not graduate high school." So, yeah, we cheated. But got our diplomas! Even had a graduation. Caps and gowns and everything.

That was sometime between ages 21 and 25. It might've have been pre-Navy? Hard to say. I don't remember the timelines exactly. But everything I've told you is *pretty much* how it happened. A *resemblance* to the truth, you know what I mean? Who could keep it all straight? I was in and out of detentions, rehabs, psychiatric wards. Was home, not home, had an apartment, left an apartment, in the military, home again. So many different changes in such a short span.

And, after all that, where was I? Thinking about the life that I wanted to live. Doing the things that I wanted to do. Everything boiled down to: money. How was I going to get enough to live? Working restaurant jobs? Menial labor? Spending all of your time doing something that you fucking hate. Only to get paid shit for it. Work 70 hours a week, you know, and then barely have time, between shifts, to do your laundry and poop. Destined to be a working class slob until you die. Bye-bye.

What kind of life is that? What's the fucking point?

THIS IS A ROBBERY!
1991-1996

New Britain, Connecticut. I was renting a room. From a woman, you know, *whose boyfriend* was in the cocaine distribution business.

This boyfriend. He and his buddy were planning to sell a kilo to some dude. They had the kilo, but decided, nah, they were going to burn the dude. Sell him a fake kilo. For some reason – who knows why? – they also brought the real kilo to the meet. It turned out: the dude was an undercover cop, and the boyfriend got *busted*. Before going to jail, though, out on bond, he unloaded all of his shit. Including a couple of snowboards. He said to me: "For $100, you can have both." So I bought the snowboards. Kept one for myself. And gave the other to my brother Mike.

I had never snowboarded before. Only skied. Growing up, we would visit this local suburban ski area called Mt. Southington. It wasn't really a mountain. Just a little hill. And Robert was an asshole, definitely, but a hard worker. He *hustled*. Worked his full-time job at IGA, but then also a part-time gig at Mt. Southington. To earn some extra money and free skiing. Me and my brother Mike would come along sometimes. Help him clean the ski lodge. Robert would give us each like $10, you know, and then we'd go skiing.

Mike is much younger than me, so were never really that close. But that changed when we started snowboarding together. I actually have a newspaper article from *The Hartford Courant*. Dated Saturday, February 20th, 1993. A reporter, I guess, had shown up at Mt. Southington to write a piece on snowboarding, and they used a picture of us for the article. My brother Mike is kneeling down. One hand in the air. And I'm on my snowboard. Soaring over him.

We'd occasionally even take overnight trips up to Mt. Killington in Vermont with Robert and Sandra. I remember, one time, veering off the trail and zipping through the woods on my snowboard. Dodging trees. When I came out, back onto the trail, Robert just happened to be skiing by. And I blasted right into him! Knocked him completely off his skis! He yelled out, "You fucking asshole!" I jumped back up on my board: "Sorry!" And took off down the mountain.

Snowboarding is now in the Olympics. In the beginning, though, it was more of this rebellious thing. The culture was adopted from surfing, skateboarding, and later, hip-hop. And it was frowned upon. There were trails on Mt. Killington that didn't even allow snowboarding! Ski resorts were traditionally these kind of buttoned-up places for rich people. They freaked out when the snowboarders hit the slopes. Which thrilled us on some level. Hell yeah. That was part of the fun.

We would snowboard all day and still not be tired. So then we'd go to grocery store parking lots and videotape ourselves doing tricks. Slide down the mounds of snow made by plows. Jump grocery carts. Ride down banisters. This is called "jibbing." Like, on the slopes, if we saw a log on the side of a hill, we would board up onto the log, do a little trick, and hop down. On one trail, you could pop up onto the roof of this storage shack and then ride off the edge. I hit that trick a few times, but the last time I tried it, I landed on my head. Caught a quick concussion.

I wasn't great at jibbing. Physics, you know, with my body size, it's difficult for me to get off the ground without the help of an apparatus. I was more into hitting jumps. At this rinky-dink place in Connecticut called Woodbury Ski and Racquet, the manager didn't care what we did. He'd give us shovels and let us build whatever we wanted.

So we'd pack snow into these big wedges. And then board down the hill really fast, up and off the wedge, through the air, and then, *hopefully*, land. Upright.

Snowboarding is the source, man. That's what this kid says to Keanu Reeves, you know, about surfing, near the beginning of *Point Break*. The feeling when you drop into a big jump. It's hard to describe. It's amazing, terrifying, exhilarating. A real free experience. There's a split second where time freezes. And you're out of this world.

*

Kelly and I were introduced by my friend Alex, the guitar player in my band. And we just hit it off. I wasn't like head over heels, but she was fun. Super cute. Easy to be around. Smoked a shit ton of weed.

The whole situation was very Connecticut. Kelly lived in Bristol. The hometown of Aaron Hernandez. She had a baby named Matthew and a Jamaican baby daddy in jail for selling drugs. In almost no time, we were living together in an apartment in Bristol. Me, Kelly, and Matthew. Even though she warned me from the start: "Danny, I really like you and all. But when my baby's father gets out of jail, I'm getting back with him."

The band? We were called Rebellious Nature! I don't play any instruments. No, I was the front man. Vocals. Alex played guitar. We never had a bass player. Every now and then, someone would sit in on the drums. Mostly, we wrote and looped beats on a drum machine. It was like… experimental. We had a lot of energy, but weren't very good. Weren't like getting ready to tour or anything. Didn't have regular band practice. Whatever. I still called it "the band."

We did play a few local venues. There was this health food restaurant where I worked, briefly, as a waiter. The owner, a real hip chick, let me rollerblade around serving tables. And she would host open mics at the restaurant. I remember, once, some jam band was on stage, you know, jamming *forever*, and I had to go up there and say, "Hey, beat it! We want to do a set." We only had like four songs. One original that I wrote. And like three Rage Against the Machine covers.

Man, when that first Rage album came out. The one with the monk on the cover. Lighting himself on fire. I listened to it over and over and over again. The last song "Freedom," you know, where Zack just screams "Freedom" at the end, inspired me to get the word "freedom" tattooed on my right forearm. And my attitude towards the police was super influenced by this music. Rage, Public Enemy, NWA. The hair on my arms still stands up when I think about hearing that for the first time. These Black guys from L.A. saying, "Fuck the police!"

The Rodney King incident was right around this time. Oh my god. Go back and watch that video. Like eight policemen standing over the man. Viciously beating him with billy clubs. While he crawls across the ground. Begging for mercy. Those motherfuckers were acquitted of any wrongdoing! They *all* got off. Which sparked the riots, you know, where like half of L.A. burned down. I remember, clearly, coming into work and saying to a fellow employee: "Let's go out to L.A!" Because I was so angered by the video. And excited by the rioting.

That was my real introduction to systemic racism. How anyone like me was automatically seen as a criminal. But crime is rarely random. Most crime is the direct result of enormous economic imbalance. Why does a tiny group of people have so much? While the majority of society is grinding away. Barely getting by. It makes you so depressed. So you use drugs and alcohol and get more and more depressed. And then try *unsuccessfully* to commit suicide. And then wash out of the Navy, haha, because of suicidal tendencies.

That's another awesome band that I was listening to in the '90s! Suicidal Tendencies. "How Will I Laugh Tomorrow When I Can't Even Smile Today." So fucking good.

*

It was my birthday. We went snowboarding at Okemo Mountain in Vermont. Mike and I woke up early to make the three-hour drive and be there when the lifts first opened. We were drinking on the ride up. Beers and coffee.

And then we were on the mountain. Hitting jumps. Doing 360s. I could even do it "fakie," you know, where you hit the jump *backwards*, spin 540 degrees, and land face forward. I had that trick dialed in. But too many beers, maybe? Anyway. I fucked it up. Landed on my shoulder. I knew something was wrong immediately, but there was no way they were putting me on a stretcher. So I rode down in a lot of pain. And also really had to take a crap. From all of that coffee and beer! Picture me. With a fucked up arm, struggling to get my snowboard gear off, so I could shit.

When I left the medical tent, my arm was in a sling. Broken collarbone. Fast forward to that night. One of our sisters worked for a convalescent home where they were having a Christmas party. The whole family went. And my brother Mike – not even of drinking age – got drunk as fuck and started acting like an asshole. I tried to put him in check, you know, but he wasn't having it. So… we got into a fistfight. Yep. I *lit his ass up* with one good arm. He was livid: "I'm going to fucking kill you! I'm going to Waterbury to get a gun!" I was like, "Cool. Let's go. I'll give you a ride."

Mike was always kind of a mama's boy. Real close with Sandra. She coddled him. Much more than she ever did me. And he loved to be around her. Like when we were kids, if she went to do errands, then he would tag along. I remember, one time, Sandra was leaving, but told Mike that he had to stay home. So he freaked out, went running after her, and jumped on the back of the van. We had this big turnaround spot in the yard, so she was turning. And…

he fell off of the van. And… she ran him over! Just like a little bit of his leg with one tire. But still.

Like me, Mike had a pretty contentious relationship with Robert. They beefed a lot. Robert and I didn't see eye-to-eye, sure, but at least I hustled. Mike was a slug. He'd sleep in. Laze around the house all day. Hit Sandra up for money. I remember he and his friend DeSean. They would hang out. Drink 40s. Smoke weed. Listen to rap. Try *to be* rappers. I would come round sometimes to roust him, you know, take him out back to chop firewood. Make him do responsible things.

He was a good kid, you know, once you got to know him. Quiet. Funny. Super loyal. Smart, but hated school as much as I did. Dropped out in the 9th grade. He would go into "the neighborhood" in Waterbury. His pants sagging like a homeboy. My friends were all suburban white boys, but Mike gravitated towards the brothers. Later on, after we started snowboarding together, he would sometimes hang out with me in Bristol. For a little while, I even got him a job at Chuck's. As a dishwasher.

We always wanted to go snowboarding, but lift tickets are expensive, you know what I mean? At this point, the health food restaurant had closed, so I found another job waiting tables at the Ground Round. They used to serve popcorn, you know, and ice cream in those little souvenir baseball helmets. The servers actually had to get the ice cream themselves. It sucked! You're already busy, dining room full of people waiting for their food, and then you have to fetch some brat-ass kid his fucking ice cream.

I was a terrible waiter, too. Couldn't handle it. Kelly was into pills. I want to say Valium. Maybe Percocet? Whatever it was, she gave me one: "It'll help you relax." So I took one. And then went to work a shift at the Ground Round. They ended up sending me home because I couldn't function on the job! I remember one of the other waitresses saying, "This dude is fucking *drowning*." And I was.

So Mike and I were working, yeah, but still didn't have enough money to snowboard *and* party on the weekends. That's when we started doing little petty crimes. As a waiter, I always had a lot of small bills from tips. And we would go into a 7-11. Walk up to the counter. Ask for cartons of cigarettes. Take out some money, you know, a big knot of one-dollar bills. Make it look like we were ready to roll. As soon as they put those cartons on the counter, though, we'd grab them, run out, jump in the car, and go, go, go.

We got beer the same way. In Connecticut, they sell beer and liquor in the same store. The liquor's in front, and beer's kept in this huge cooler in the back. So we'd walk into the cooler, each grab a 30-rack, and pull that same stunt at the counter. One time, we were walking *towards* the counter, but then shot straight for the door. Bypassed the counter entirely. I just ran out with the beer, and Mike was right behind me. Mike's friend DeSean was in the driver's seat of my car with the trunk open. And then I heard: "Oh shit!" Mike had tripped over the curb. Sent his 30-rack flying.

There were silver cans everywhere. Spinning and leaking beer into the street. Mike's tumbling on the ground. The owner of the place was now chasing after us. I threw my beer into the trunk and jumped in the car. DeSean started driving away before Mike could even get all the way in. His legs were dangling out the door! I was laughing my ass off, man. That'll be a fun scene to shoot when we do the movie.

*

They're in the back of a van. On their way to do one last job. And right when they're about to put on their masks, Bodhi says to Johnny Utah: "Why be a servant to the law when you can be its fucking master?"

We rented *Point Break*, I remember, on VHS from the Blockbuster Video in Bristol. And then watched it *a lot* of times. It was kind of like our Bible. I can still recite almost all of the lines. Keanu Reeves as FBI agent Johnny Utah.

Way before he did *John Wick* or *The Matrix*. And Patrick Swayze – God rest his soul – as Bodhi. The rebellious surfer. And the leader of this bank robbing crew. They wore ex-presidents masks and would rob banks, every summer, you know, just so they could surf.

Mike and I saw ourselves in that movie. Definitely. They wanted it to be never winter. We wanted it to be never summer. Just go where the snow is and not have to work. And their whole philosophy. There's one speech where everyone is sitting around a campfire on the beach. Bodhi says, "This was never about money for us. It was about us against the system. That system that kills the human spirit. We stand for something. To those dead souls inching along the freeway in their metal coffins, we show them that human spirit is still alive." Well, there you go!

It wasn't about the money itself. Money is not the end. Freedom from bondage is the end. From the belief that you have to trudge away. Wake up every day. Get into your metal coffin and drive to your job. If you want to earn a buck. If you want to have food and clothes. If you want to live indoors. Then you have to be part of this system that doesn't give a shit about you. Working yourself half to death. And that's what Bodhi is talking about. That's not living. That's the death of your spirit.

So *Point Break* planted the seed. And then, one winter night, we were driving around in the neighborhood of Chuck's. When my brother noticed it. This ritzy Buick LeSabre. Money green. We knew the car. It belonged to this old fat white guy who ran some architectural firm. He would come into Chuck's and drink at the bar for hours and hours with his friends. The idiot. He would park right in front of the restaurant and leave his car running. To keep it warm while he got drunk. Sure enough, that night, when we checked, the car was running. So… we stole it.

At the time, in Connecticut, you could have just one plate on your car. It wouldn't raise any eyebrows if you only had a rear license plate. And there are a ton of commuter parking lots in Connecticut. Because the rich Connecticut people all work in New York City. So we removed the plate, took the stolen car to one of these Park n' Rides, and backed it into a spot. Left it there. For weeks. Whenever we wanted to do something crazy, we would go back and get it. Push it around like it was ours.

We were in the LeSabre *that day*. I didn't even really tell my brother what I was planning to do, but he knew I was up to something. I put on this black wig underneath my snowboarding hat. Pulled my neck cozy up, so you could only see a little bit of my face. In my lap, I was holding a sawed-off double-barreled shotgun. I had Mike park in some plaza and said, "Wait here. I'll be right back."

I crossed the street and walked into the bank. I expected to burst in: "Alright. Everybody get down!" But didn't have the balls. So I just kind of… waited in line. In my wig, you know, with all of this snowboarding gear on. The shotgun up my sleeve. Inching my way towards the counter. And when the teller said, "Can I help who's next?" That's when I made my move. Stepped from the line. Announced: "This is a robbery!" Ran, jumped, shotgun in one hand, my other hand on the counter for support, and landed. Over the counter in one leap!

It's such a weird experience to actually rob a bank. The adrenaline is intense. And everything in your psyche tells you that you should not be doing this. You could get in so much trouble and so many things could go wrong. But as soon as you yell: "This is a robbery!" That's it, man. You're in a bubble where this is the only thing happening. And you have to do it. And you do it. And then you get out. And then *whoosh*. Your brain turns back on.

I jumped back in the car: "Go! Go! Go!" My brother's eyes bugged out of his head when he saw the sack-full-of-cash! It was only like $2,500. Because I only hit one drawer and ran. I had no idea what the fuck I was doing. That was the first time, you know, and then we literally drove directly from the bank. To Vermont. And went snowboarding.

*

That first job, I think, was a People's Bank. A local bank in Connecticut. Their slogan was: "We're *your* bank." So we used to joke: "Alright then. Give us *our* money."

After that, I quit my waiter job at the fucking Ground Round. So now we could just hang out, drink, smoke weed, snowboard, and do whatever we wanted. And whenever our funds got low, you know, we would plot a new job. I don't remember a lot of the details. Especially once everything started happening, most of the robberies blur together. But the banks we hit were all over Connecticut. Farther and farther away from Bristol. Southington. Watertown. Manchester.

Like any kind of artistic expression, there was a certain amount of improvisation, but we also began to develop some rules. For instance. Pick a spot close to the highway. So you can get the fuck out of town fast. And don't pull up directly in front of the bank. Park somewhere that, within a reasonable amount of time, moving at a pretty good stride, but not looking weird, you can walk to the bank. I liked to find a parking lot nearby with a big shrubbery wall. So I could escape through the shrubberies, and if anybody had anything to report, then all they could say is: "The guy left *on foot.*"

Door to door. Sixty seconds. So even if the bank teller pushes an alarm as soon as they hear: "This is a robbery!" And a call goes out: "Robbery-in-progress at such and such an address." There's a pretty low chance that any officer can be on the scene within 60 seconds. When a robbery happens, the police go straight to the bank. If you can get-in-and-get-out, then by the time police arrive and start collecting information, their information is already pointless. Because that shit is over. You're on the highway. Driving away.

We did park in front sometimes, but only when we had a "switch car." Eventually, you know, we had a little fleet of stolen cars, on ice, sitting in various commuter parking lots. And whenever we needed another car, we'd wait outside of a gas station or convenient store. In the bushes. Dressed in black. With walkie-talkies and binoculars. We thought we were like commandos! And if someone went in and left their car running, we would pop out of the bushes, hop in the car, and drive.

So we would pull up to a bank in one car, get-in-and-get-out, quickly change clothes, drive that car a few blocks away, leave it there, and jump into a switch car. And then drive, very casually, out of town. There were times when we'd be stopped at a light, waiting for it to turn. Mike behind the wheel, and me, slinking way down in the passenger seat. The cops would come racing past us, the other way, towards the bank. Sirens blaring: "Whoooo! Whoooo!" And we'd just be chuckling. Thinking that shit was funny as hell.

Yeah, my brother was the driver, and I was the inside man. I mean, we were rolling around in stolen cars. And Mike is, um… white. So he wouldn't stick out, you know what I mean? Like when was the last time you were pulled over for any kind of traffic violation? It doesn't happen to white people very often. If you just chill, drive normally, and pay attention to the road. But I don't know if you've heard. Black people get pulled over every damn day. For no fucking reason at all.

Also, for the record, I was against using guns. You don't really need a gun to do the job itself. All you want is for the people in the bank to be afraid. And if you just *tell* people that you have a gun, then they'll be afraid. We were never looking to harm any civilians. For some of the early jobs, actually, I used a plastic toy gun from a box store. Ripped off the orange thing, you know, and it was good to go. However. If the police came for us, then we thought that we should be somewhat prepared.

Because we decided early on: we were not getting caught. That was always our attitude. Do-or-die. Either see this thing through all the way. Or death by cop. Like Butch Cassidy and the Sundance Kid. A couple of romantics. When their backs were against the wall. Running straight into the fire. And then: outlaw heaven.

*

When Kelly finally put two and two together, you know, found out that we were robbing banks, she was very... turned on. Literally asked to be inside the bank on our next job. Wanted to watch. I was like, "O-kay! You down ass bitch!" Yeah, Kelly was *hanging out*. She and her son, Matthew. Now, a toddler. Almost two years old. He and I were buds. One morning, though, we woke up, and he was walking around with my little .22 pistol in his hands. That was like, "Whoa! We need to start paying attention."

So, yeah, I did end up with a couple of pistols: a .38 and a .22. Like I said, fake guns won't shoot you out of a tight spot. Plus, they both really wanted guns. My brother and the other kid that started working with us. Brent McCall. Classic outlaw name. Looked like a mellow dude. You would never imagine that he was a violent lunatic. Read *The Anarchist Cookbook*. Made pipe bombs. Had a weird thing about cops. He told us about how his brother had been shot *to death* by the Bristol police. I don't know if that story is true. I never really knew Brent that well.

He knew Kelly, and she would invite him over to the apartment. One night, we were all drinking beers, and Brent started talking about this scam. Where you start a phony small business. Falsify documents. And then go up to Canada with all of this fake information, approach a bank, and get a loan. Take the money, you know, but then just default on the loan. I was like, "Hmmmm. Interesting. But we do it different." And then Mike and I got braggadocious. Brent wanted to join up with us right away. Logistically, it's definitely easier with a third person, so we brought him aboard.

How we got the guns. That's a story in itself. My brother knew this girl *whose boyfriend* had access to guns. But the boyfriend was currently jammed up, sitting in jail, and she was trying to raise money for his bail. She had a plan… to rob a truck stop. We were skeptical: "How much money could there possibly be? It's a convenient store." But she had specific information: "No. The *fuel desk* at the 76. They have thousands and thousands of dollars back there." So we said, "Alright. Here's the deal. Because you brought this to us, we'll give you a cut. To bail out your boyfriend. And then he'll give us some guns."

The 76 Truck Stop in Southington. When I was a kid, we'd go there sometimes to eat at the diner. That day, we pulled up in a stolen pickup truck. My brother was driving. Me and Brent were in the back. We jumped out and burst through the doors: "This is a robbery!" Immediately, the situation was pretty sketchy. First of all, there was a security guard. And the window to the fuel desk was tiny. So Brent went diving through the window, while I kept an eye on the security guard. Pointed my sawed-off double-barreled shotgun: "Get the fuck on the ground!"

The security guard got on the ground. We were in this wide open area, and I wasn't comfortable *at all*. So I walked down to one end, looked around the corner, towards the convenient store. No one there. Nothing going on. But when I looked back, the security guard had gotten up and taken off. And when I looked out the window, to check on Mike, there was now an empty cop car parked out there, too. I yelled, "Yo, man! It's time to go! Police!"

So Brent dove back over the fuel desk with a shit ton of money. And then we ran, you know, away from where we had originally entered. Through the convenient store. The clerk was on the phone, and I started screaming, "Hang up the phone! Hang up the phone!" Showing her my shotgun.

She looked at me like I was crazy, and I tripped right over the sunglasses rack. The shotgun went off. Fired into the ceiling. So now – boom! – shots fired! At an armed robbery-in-progress.

The convenient store opened into the diner, and when we ran in, there were like twelve guys in what-looked-to-be police uniforms. Running *away from us*. I was like, "Oh shit! Cops!" But they weren't cops. It was a group of COs. Correctional officers. Having lunch at the diner. They must have freaked out when they heard the gunshot. Because they cleared the fuck out. And we sprinted through the diner, out through a different exit, through the woods out back, and around to the other side. Where Mike was waiting in the truck. We hopped in and hauled ass.

We met up at a hotel. To give that girl her cut of the loot. And then, when her boyfriend was out of jail, we met up again to get our guns. Dude wanted to *charge us* for the guns. I looked at the girl: "No way. That wasn't the deal. We risked our lives to bail him out. He was supposed to *give us* guns." I wanted to beat them both up, I swear, the girl and her boyfriend. But my brother and Brent were like, "C'mon, Danny. Who cares?" They were just so excited to now have guns.

Shortly after, we went to a place in the woods to practice shooting. By a little brook and a reservoir, there was a bunch of geese. Brent suggested that we practice on the geese. So we snuck up over a hill and started shooting. Almost immediately, I felt terrible. Why the fuck would we want to kill some innocent geese? We could have used anything for target practice. It was probably 25 years ago, and to this day, I still feel bad about shooting those geese. Who were just like hanging out. Being geese.

*

That year, I remember, the song "1st of Tha Month" by Bone Thugs-N-Harmony was really popular. I had the cassette single in my car and played that shit *too many times*. It was the soundtrack to all of our movements around and across Connecticut.

We moved to an apartment in Hartford, you know, in the hood. Where we wouldn't be noticed as much. Where we wouldn't stick out. Nobody would care. If we didn't go to work. Partied all day. People came in and out of that apartment, Mike's friends and Brent's friends, but most of the time, it was the six of us. Kelly and I, Brent and his girlfriend, and then Brent's girlfriend's friend. And Mike. He didn't *really* like this chick, but they ended up hanging out a lot. And sometimes sleeping together, you know, because.

At one point, Brent and his girlfriend drove down to D.C. for a few days. And when they returned, he told us a story. How they were driving through Pennsylvania, and a state trooper followed them for like an hour and a half. I was like, "Yo! We're bank robbers! Carrying illegal firearms! We should be laying low! You're going to get yourself into a situation that'll be frustrating. For everyone involved."

But we were running out of money. So I came up with a plan: "Let's hit 'em hard. Do two jobs in one day. Get a decent amount of dough. *And then lay low*. Go our separate ways for a while. Until we figure out our next move." So we scouted out some banks north and south of Hartford. We decided to hit one bank in Avon, get on the highway, drive to Meriden, and hit another bank. While the police were scrambling to find out what the hell was going on, we'd already be back in Hartford. Chilling.

And that's what we did. That morning, we brought the switch car – which was actually my car, an old Buick Regal registered to me – down to Meriden and parked it in a hotel lot near the bank. And then we left in a stolen minivan and drove to do the first job in Avon. It was a super small bank, and we didn't get that much money. Only a couple of grand. We were definitely not thrilled with that result. But kept with the plan and headed back to Meriden.

When we arrived at the little plaza where the bank was located, a police car was circling the parking lot. So we retreated, drove down the road a bit, and took stock. Finally, I said, "Fuck it." And proposed that we do the job anyway. In retrospect, of course, that was crazy! There was a cop right there! Why didn't we just scrap the whole thing? I have no idea. But we didn't. And when we turned back into the plaza, lucky us, the police car was now nowhere to be seen.

So my brother waited in the minivan. While Brent and I went into the bank. I was on crowd control, watching the lobby, and Brent was over the counter, going through the drawers. If you're on crowd control then you're also on time control. About 45 seconds in, Brent found the *main* teller drawer. The drawer they use to replenish all of the other drawers. He was like, "Holy shit!" And I was like, "Alright! C'mon! C'mon! We're almost out of time!" Brent filled the bag with as much money as he could grab, and we ran out of the bank. No police anywhere.

Mike exited the plaza. He was being cool behind the wheel, and Brent and I were in the back of the minivan. Counting the money. And there was *a lot* of fucking money! Over $50,000. This was the score that we had been waiting for. But then – "what the fuck?!!!!" – red smoke began pouring out of the bag. There had been a fucking dye-pack in the drawer. The smoke was burning our eyes and filling the entire minivan. We could hear police sirens in the distance. My brother was driving with his head like *out the window*. Trying like hell to get us to the switch car.

He didn't even pull into the lot where the switch car was parked. Just went flying over the big curb, you know, with the rocks and little trees and shit. And when we landed – "ba-boom!" – they jumped out and bolted towards my Buick. I was like, "Guys! Hold on!" The shotgun was still in the minivan. With a giant fucking pile of smoldering money. We grabbed whatever we could, ran to the switch car, and peeled out. On the highway, cops flew by in the opposite direction, and we knew the coast was clear.

Most of our booty was ruined, but we did salvage some of that money. Put the bills in the bathtub and lightened them up with bleach. After the dye-pack incident, though, we were all a little on edge. Maybe that's why Brent did what he did. A few weeks later, he pulled into his girlfriend's driveway in Bristol. And then a cop pulled in behind him. There had been a domestic violence call, I guess, at the house *next door*. But Brent must have thought that they had come for him. So he freaked out. Didn't even hesitate. Jumped out of the car. And just started shooting.

*

They didn't have cell phones back then. Well, at least, we didn't have cell phones. But I got a message from Brent on my pager: "9-1-1. 9-1-1." That didn't sound good. I didn't find out the details until later. By watching the news!

So Brent got jammed up and that was a wrap for him. He'll probably never come home. Dude shot a cop! Seriously wounded a police officer. Brent himself was shot, too, and then ran around Bristol. Trying to make an escape. They eventually caught him after a massive manhunt. The whole thing was crazy. But, to be honest, I was mostly just annoyed. He fucking burned us. Turned up the heat.

The police found some stuff in Brent's car that put him in connection with the recent string of bank robberies. And his girlfriend had fled from the scene. Straight to Kelly's house. And somebody had seen his girlfriend go there. So when they eventually caught her, they wanted to question Kelly, too. I actually drove Kelly – in my own car – to the fucking FBI field office in Bristol. Dropped her off. Right outside.

She didn't break. They *kind of* knew that Kelly had been dating some guy who *might* also be involved with the bank robberies. But they didn't really have anything. And Kelly was a trooper! Imagine being a girl in your 20s with a young son. Your drug-dealing husband is in jail. You're dating a bank robber. And you're sitting there in an interrogation room. Saying: "He was just a guy I was dating. I don't know where he is now. Last I heard, he was going out west." She said this. Over and over. For hours! To the FBI!

Kelly walked out of that office and called from a payphone a few blocks away. I picked her up, and then, you know, we went about our business. The authorities still didn't know anything about me and my brother. So it was just the two of us, again, and we started planning another job. Was that fucking crazy? Probably. At that point, though, the robberies themselves really didn't make me nervous. We had already hit so many banks and never had an issue. What was one more?

I had this idea. Kelly went to an art supply store and bought me a block of gray molding clay. And then I took a radar detector that we had ripped from a stolen car. Put it on top of the clay. With a 9-volt battery and a bunch of wires. Taped it all up, you know, so it looked like an explosive device. If you just tell someone that you have a bomb, then they're going to fucking comply. No questions asked. That was my thinking.

Liberty Bank in Cromwell, Connecticut. I entered, walked right up to the teller, put the fake bomb on the counter, and explained, "This is a bomb. If you don't do everything I say, then I'm going to blow this place to bits." From out of my peripheral vision, I saw the drive-through teller approaching. Stacks of bills in each hand: "Here you go, sir." Dude just handed me the money. Very compliantly.

I walked out of that bank with an easy $20,000! And people who read this will probably think I'm an asshole, but what really sticks out in my memory is watching the news that night. Seeing the police show up to the bank with the bomb squad. That guy, you know, in the big suit. Exploding my harmless little art project in his bomb box. I thought that was fucking hilarious.

*

I was just googling "the Killion brothers." Trying to jog some memories. And I found a couple of newspaper articles. One from *The Hartford Courant*. Dated July 10th, 1996. It says that we did seven bank robberies in all. And, yes, we got convicted for seven. So... that's how many we did.

It also says the first robbery was on March 8th and the last was on June 4th. That's less than three months! Officially, I think we can call that a "spree"! Man, it sure seems like longer in my mind, but I guess that makes sense. Because we started in the winter. Literally left that first job in the stolen Buick LeSabre and went snowboarding in Vermont. And when we got caught, it was summertime. We had just left the beach.

Bank robbing, at least back then, turned out to be easy as fuck. We might never have been caught if we just kept the operation to ourselves and didn't involve anyone else. Although Brent never told anyone anything. And Brent's girlfriend never talked, either. But... Brent's girlfriend's friend. The cops found a fucking bundle of heroin on her. Jackpot. Right away, you know, she was like, "Oh, I definitely know some shit!" And gave us up. Without blinking.

As soon as that chick got busted, I knew it was time to get the fuck out of Dodge. My plan was for Mike and I to go down to Florida. Maybe buy a small boat. Live on the boat. Cruise up and down the coast. On the run from the feds. Whenever we needed money, you know, we could park the boat in a marina. Come into any little town. Rob a few banks. Get back on the boat. Sail away. Kelly was like, "So I'll probably never see you again?" And I was like, "No. Probably not."

So we decided to spend one more full day together. In New London, Connecticut. Ocean Beach Park. Me, Mike, Kelly, and Matthew. I can still picture the little dude in the backseat of my Regal. Bobbing his head to the hip-hop. We were at the beach all day. Swimming in the ocean. Lying in the sun. I remember making a sand castle and writing "FBI" on the top. And then having a nice dinner at Chuck's Steakhouse. The New London location. I was drinking Snakebites. Yukon Jack and lime juice.

At the beach, I had seen a flyer. Someone selling a boat. For $2,500, you know, exactly like the one I imagined. So, on the way out of town, we pulled into a gas station, and I went over to a payphone to inquire about the boat. My car had a little leak, so I asked Mike to check the oil. I was at the payphone, and Mike had the hood up. Kelly was in the backseat with Matthew. As I was talking on the phone, a bicycle cop came riding through the lot. Looked in the windows of our car. Walked around back. Inspected the plate. Hopped on his bike and rode away.

I remember, distinctly, how I stopped hearing what the guy on the phone was saying. And then how I came-to, a second later, hanging up the phone. I walked-ran to the car: "Mike, shut the hood! Let's go!" By the time he put the hood down, though, they had already swarmed in. We weren't even in the car yet, and the place was full of cops! And then there was a gun right to the back of my head: "Freeze!"

Mike's pistol was in the front seat. My pistol was right there in my waistband. But I looked through the car window into the backseat. At Kelly. And Matthew. Who was looking up at me. And then I put my hands behind my back. Busted!

CONGRATULATIONS ASSHOLE

1996-2007

When we had moved to Hartford, I began using the alias "Paul Blackman." Paul like the apostle from the New Testament. Before he was Christian, that dude went around *murdering* Christians. Just because they were Christian. Until Jesus appeared to him on the road, and then all of his Christian-murdering was forgiven. I always thought that was pretty interesting, so I named myself Paul... Blackman, you know, like Black man.

And when we got busted, I had a fake ID on me with the name Paul Blackman. So, on my initial intake at county jail, they processed me as Paul Blackman! I said, "No, man. You guys are dumb as shit. That's not my real name." But they were like, "Nope. That's your name, asshole." And that's what the fuck they called me. For the whole time that I was stuck in the Connecticut state prison system. Inmate 174803: Paul Blackman.

The Hartford County Correctional Center. We sat there for months, waiting, while our various charges were sorted out. And when I arrived, after letting the police take me alive, I alluded to the possibility that I might kill myself. So they put me on suicide watch. Private cell. Paper gown. I remember wondering: "If I stood on the bed, and dove towards the toilet, headfirst, maybe I would die?" There's a video on the internet of a prisoner who did that, and it's pretty fucking horrific. I'm glad I never tried!

When I calmed down a little, they moved me to a regular cellblock. But county jail... sucks. It's bare and broken-down and loud. Rats and spit everywhere. Because nobody gives a fuck. No one's doing any real time there. Although there were also a ton of human beings packed into that place, and everyone was fucking insane. The majority were people from the hood involved in the crack game. A gritty type of human being. Like I didn't get into many fights in prison, but at county, it just happens.

There was no chow hall. So you didn't leave your cell block for breakfast. They rolled around this cart with one tray for each person. And they popped the doors, mad early, like 5:30, and then you sat in this little tiny space to eat. Two hard-boiled eggs, super runny oatmeal, and some white toast. So we'd all get up, eat that shit, and then return to our cells. Lock in, lie down, go back to sleep.

One guy, however, would always miss breakfast. And then bang on the door. Yell for the CO: "Yo, let me out. I want breakfast!" But listen, man. Breakfast is fucking over. And now we're all trying to sleep. So you need to shut the fuck up. That's what I said to him, you know, respectfully. And he said, "Well, I must not be bothering anyone. Because my face ain't yet fucked up." I remember taking off my shower shoes. So I wouldn't slip. And then smacking him as hard as I could: "Powwww!" Dude kept quiet after that.

My brother was in county with me, but in a different cellblock. Usually, when you're co-defendants, they'll split you up. I'd only get to see him on court trips. Which were the worst. They wake you up at 4:00 in the morning and take you down to the bullpen. You wait there with the 10-15 other prisoners heading to the same court. You're shackled and belly-chained together and loaded into the back of a van. And then court trips take *all day*. Many times, nothing even happens. No decisions. No agreements. So you'd have to come back some other day. Do the whole thing over again.

We were driven around and around, man. To the different courthouses in the different towns where we robbed banks. And if there had been actual trials, which would have taken forever, we could have been found guilty at all of them. One place could have said, "We're going to charge them with *this*." And another place could have said, "We're going to charge them with *this*." And if we were found guilty each time – 25 years a pop – then we might have done life in prison.

Moreover, if you rob a bank in a state, then that state can charge you with the crime. But bank robbing is also a federal crime. Because banks are federally insured. *Most of the time*, you'll only get charged by the feds, but Connecticut came after us hard. Eventually, everything was bundled together. Our public defender talked to the prosecutors. Made a deal. We'd plead guilty. They'd drop some of the charges. And agree on concurrent sentences: 157 months total. We'd serve nine years in Connecticut and finish out our time at a federal facility.

Considering, you know, the shit that we did, it seemed like a pretty light sentence. That's what I thought. But my brother was upset. He thought that we should have fought some of the charges. And felt like he got bullied into taking the plea bargain. He was just fucking deluded. Like dude. We robbed banks! With illegal firearms! They found stolen money in our pockets! You're not beating those charges.

We were sentenced in the fall. At a federal courthouse in New Haven. A few people showed up to give statements on our behalf. Sandra. Our oldest sister Sheri. The judge said something about how we seemed like decent guys. Who were battling psychological issues. Alcohol and substance abuse. Blah blah blah. Yeah, we kind of played that up, you know, after we were caught. Anything to get less time.

But a bank teller was also in court that day. The one from the very first robbery. And she gave a statement, too. This white woman in her 20s. She recalled how, when I put my shotgun in her face, she had peed her pants. And she was crying: "I still have nightmares."

*

I was sent to a maximum security prison. Cheshire Correctional Institution. There was an old section and a new section. The old section still looked like prisons did back in the day. Brick and mortar. Metal bars on the windows. This is where they kept you during the intake process until they decided what to do with you.

Weirdly, during my first few days in intake, I became very... environmentally-minded. Concerned. About how much garbage the jail was generating on a daily basis. Maybe I was just being rebellious? I don't know. But imagine. There were hundreds and hundreds of dudes in that prison. And every single day, for every single meal, they gave us disposable stuff to eat with. I was like, "Do the math on that shit! That's a lot of garbage." And then I threatened to go on a hunger strike.

Smart plan, right? What a fucking idiot! Like here I am. Potentially doing nine years in this place and starting trouble right away. That lasted about a month. I remember being pulled from my cell and brought before the brass. Who told me: "Hey. Just fucking cut it out. We're not changing anything. And you're getting under our skin. If you don't quit this crusade, we'll send you to seg. Or put you in the hole. *Until you die.*"

So I gave up on that shit and was moved to a cell block. Where, right away, I was just super eccentric. My own unique self, you know what I mean? Like picture a cell block. There's a lower level of cells and an upper level of cells lined with a railing. The CO's desk is raised in the middle. From there, half flights of stairs lead up and down. And a full flight of stairs connects the top and bottom. With my snowboarder's mentality, I saw... possibilities. For all kinds of crazy stunts!

I'd walk up the stairs on my hands. Run from the top platform, jump, spin over the railing, do some fancy trick in the air, glance off of the industrial furniture, and try to stick the landing. I did this kind of shit *everyday*. It was like prison Parkour. Other inmates would be all confused:

"What the fuck is wrong this dude?" There was a guy named Ghost. One day, early on, Ghost was like, "Wow! You're wild, man!" And that's what they started calling me around the block. Wildman.

We were cooped up all day, you know, so whenever there was a chance to be out on the block, I got super hyper. The roughest part of maximum security prison, definitely, was the 24-hour lockdown. You came out of your cell to shower and to eat. Half hour for breakfast. Half hour for lunch. Half hour for dinner. And then, at some point during the day, you also got one hour of rec time. That was it.

When you did get to go outside for rec, you weren't allowed to run down the halls. But everyone wanted to be the first one to the basketball court. Because a lot of guys wanted to play. And there were only so many spots. And only so much time. So dudes would do that awkward walk-run to get the first game. Or next. It was a whole fucking fiasco! There were always critics, arguments, fouls, fights. Someone would get mad. Kick the ball over the fence. It was usually no fun at all.

And, other than that, you had to entertain yourself in the cell. Read. Draw. Play cards. Play chess. Some dudes would lie down and watch TV *all day*. It was funny. I liked the top bunk. So I'd be on the top, and my celly – cellmate – would be on the bottom. And we'd have two televisions. One on a desk and another on a shelf right above the desk. And we'd both have headphones on, wires crisscrossing the cell, so we could watch TV at the same time. No cable, either. Just the basic channels. What did we watch? Sports. Shitty syndicated sitcoms. Fucking Jerry Springer. "Jerry! Jerry! Jerry!"

We would eat right outside of our cells in a common area. They would wheel in the food carts. You'd stand in line with a tray. And they'd give you your meal and utensils. Plastic. Of course! What kind of moron would give metal silverware to prisoners?

*

I hardly saw my brother Mike at Cheshire. They *claimed* that we were plotting an escape. I don't know what fucking jailhouse snitch said that, but that's what they heard. So Mike and I weren't allowed to be cellies. We weren't even allowed on the same block.

You can request a celly. At the beginning, though, it was challenging. Because I was just thrown in a cell with whomever. My first cellmate: John. He was a weird guy. Obviously, mentally challenged. Hardcore Christian. In jail for sexually abusing his own son. He tried to say to me: "You don't understand. I was sexually abused as a child." But I was like, "I don't care, man. Sort that out with your fucking god. When I'm here, just sit on your bunk. And don't speak." And then I turned up the Slayer.

When I first got to prison, I tried reading the Bible. And, during rec, some inmates organized their own Bible study. It was run by a dude named Rice. This really heavy brother. He always had a jovial demeanor and responded to everything: "Yes. Blessed." So my celly John would attend this Bible study. And I went *one time*. I remember Rice getting mad at me. Because I was like, "Yo! We have a fucking child molester here!" And Rice was like, "Hey, leave John alone. It's God's choice to forgive."

So I toyed with that idea for a while. Until this other guy named Justice took John's Walkman. And I said to him: "That's fucked up, man. Give John back his Walkman." And Justice called me into his cell: "Yo, Wildman. That dude's a fucking child molester." And I was like, "Yeah. But isn't it up to God to judge him?" And Justice was like, "No! It's up *to us.*" And that felt more right to me. Even criminals pretty much agree, you know, there should be swift and harsh punishment for certain things.

Most of the time, you won't know exactly what guys are in for. But, at some point, you have to like... present.

If you're new on the block, and nobody knows you, then someone will come up and say, "It's time to 'check in.' We need to see your paperwork." And that means: the community needs to be sure. That you're not a child molester. Or a rat. You have to share your case with at least one person. Or word gets around.

It usually has something to do with violence, guns, or drugs. Usually weed, you know what I mean? And now weed is fucking legal. Those people should be let out! We have over 2,000,000 people incarcerated in this country – 2,000,000! – and like 70% of them are Black or Hispanic. That's the way it was at Cheshire. That's the way it is everywhere in the United States! Because Black and brown people, you know, we're more criminally-minded than white people. C'mon.

Don't get me wrong. I'm not saying that we need to open all of the doors and let everyone back into society. There are some bad people. For instance. At Cheshire, there was an old guy named Smokey. He had been working at a factory. Living in a trailer somewhere. Hired a hooker to come over to his house. But then didn't want to pay the hooker, so… he killed her. Kept her dead body around for a while. And then eventually shoved her under his trailer. Okay. We definitely don't want him walking around!

Funny story though. Smokey met Bubba along the way. And Bubba decided to make Smokey his wife. Nobody wanted to be in the shower with Smokey. Because he couldn't hold his bowels. I'm sorry. Maybe it's not funny. But unless you talk with someone who has been incarcerated, it might not cross your mind. That there was an old man who murdered a hooker and then got raped so often that he shat himself in the shower. This is something that happened. In our human culture.

*

Once you're in the prison system, then you just have to start... doing your time. Settle in. Get a routine. Try to find a job.

The jobs in a maximum security prison are pretty slim. If you do find work, then it's probably in the kitchen. I worked there for a while. When you get a job in the kitchen, they move you to a cell block of only kitchen workers. So I got a new cell and a new celly. And was on this really small crew. We had to wake up at 2:00 in the morning, go down to the kitchen, and get everything ready for breakfast.

I was the baker. Although I use that term *loosely*. They served these no-nutrients-not-sure-what-the-fuck-it-is pieces of cake. On the tray next to your oatmeal. I would dump this big bag of powder into the mixer, add water, and press a button. Didn't even add any egg. Just poured the watery mix into pans. And slid the pans into this giant rotating oven. I made tray after tray after tray of this shit and called it "baking."

I was paid $6 a week, you know, a dollar a day to spend at the commissary. Not a lot of money, but at least you had some freedom of movement. And we were like vicious smugglers. All of the food left the kitchen on carts. So we would steal tons of shit. Bananas, chicken, pizza, whatever. Wrap it up and hide it on the bottom of the carts. And then COs would search the carts. There was like this whole smuggler and anti-smuggler cat-and-mouse game going on in the kitchen.

One prison staffer in particular. A supervisor named Bates. We all hated that dude. What an awful fucker. He would always check the carts. Many of the other supervisors didn't care. Like if you want to steal a couple of extra hard-boiled eggs, then go ahead. Who gives a shit? But Bates. He was such a hardline power-tripping asshole. I would literally fantasize that some released inmate would find out where he lived. Show up at his door. Punch him square in the face.

He ended up getting me fired from the kitchen. I don't know if you know this, but if you take nutmeg *in large portions*, then it has a *somewhat* psychedelic effect. It's true. So, occasionally, we would get into the kitchen supplies and take a bunch of nutmeg. And, one day, we were kind of fucked up, you know, and there was only one bathroom in the kitchen. People would go in there, barricade the door with milk crates, and smoke cigarettes.

So, that day, guys were in the bathroom smoking, and I really had to pee. I looked around the kitchen and found an empty vinegar jug. And peed in it. And then motherfucking Bates busted me. Fucked up on nutmeg. Holding a jug of my own pee. He tried to make it seem like I was going to do something nefarious *with my piss*. Like put it in the food or something? I tried to tell them: "Yo, that's crazy!" But it didn't matter. They sent me to seg for two weeks.

The worst part. When you go to seg, you lose your job, lose your celly, and lose your routine. You have to start all over again.

*

When I worked in the kitchen, I had a celly named Durant. He was super intelligent. Read voraciously. Our cell was full of books. Dude only pulled out his TV once a week. Sunday nights, you know, to watch *The Simpsons*. And, in the rec yard, he would just run. Sometimes for the entire hour. But then he would also go on these long heroin binges. And then have to detox. Be in his bed shaking for days.

It was my buddy Durant who turned me on to Siddha yoga. Meditation. Yoga for the mind. There's a specific program that's free to prisoners. They send you new reading material every few weeks. And, at times, meditating, in a maximum security prison cell, I was the happiest that I'd ever been in my entire life. It's easy to sit on your pity-pot and feel bad for yourself, you know, but Siddha yoga alters your perspective. Helps you find some inner peace. Despite the circumstances.

Later, at Cheshire, I also became involved with Native American services. I had a celly who I met playing basketball. This 6'5" First Nations kid named Miguel. And he told me, if you had a little commissary money, then you could order smudging materials. For indigenous peoples, you know, certain plants are considered sacred. Sage. Palo Santo. Even tobacco. So you get a conch shell. Pack some herbs in there, and... light it up. Supposedly, the smoke purifies your soul. And carries your prayers up to the ancestors.

In the wintertime, you weren't allowed outside. Period. No rec yard or anything. Think about that. Not being able to go outdoors *at all* for months! But... if you signed up for Native American services, every morning, before breakfast, a CO would come around and pop your door. And let you out into this little fenced-in area. I always thought that was really special. To have that spiritual time. I would rise while it was still dark. Do a half hour of Siddha yoga. And then go outside into the cold. And smudge.

Once a month, too, they'd hold a sweat lodge. That was pretty dope! We would fast for three days. And then it'd be this whole day event. We'd make a fire. Put rocks on the fire. Pray while we waited for the rocks to get hot. And then build the lodge. With saplings, you know, bent over, twisted together, and covered with thick blankets. And then we'd huddle inside this structure to meditate. The heat was so intense. It felt like your skin was melting off. But when you came out, it felt amazing. Like being reborn.

Yeah, I might not have survived prison without some of these programs. Like, a couple of years into my sentence, I was let into the prison art program. You had to put in a request and be on a waiting list. And then only like a dozen inmates were allowed in the program at a time. So when I was finally accepted, it was very exciting. To be a part of this community of people interested in being creative.

That's where I met Jeff Green. An incredible human being. And a huge influence in my life. He's a tall dude. Super skinny. Floppy hair. Kind of a beatnik attitude. He went to art school for painting, but is also a musician. His band is called The Butterflies of Love. They've actually had major record sales *in England*. Their music is like whiny Brit pop. I think it's fucking awful! For the past 35 years, though, he's also been teaching art to prisoners across Connecticut. And I was immediately impressed, you know, with anyone who would do that.

In class, mostly, Jeff talked. About art. About life. About society. And then he gave us colored pencils, and pens, and paper. At first, I did a lot of pretty bad drawings. But with *extremely* intricate shading. I had so much time on my hands, you know, so I would sit in my cell for hours. Listen to music. And draw. These horned creatures. With chains on their arms and legs. They were like demons. Mad that they were being demonized. Just for being exactly who God created them to be.

So, yeah, I drew this whole series of angry demons. But then some of them were like... transformed. Into robots and octopuses and shit.

*

You never really get used to being incarcerated. But just when I was somewhat comfortable at Cheshire, they transferred me somewhere else. And you have no idea *when* or *where* you're being transferred. You don't receive any information at all. Until they pop your cell and tell you to pack your shit. That's literally what they'd say: "Blackman! Pack your shit!"

Mike had already been shipped out of Cheshire. The state prison system was *too full*. No joke. So they sent dozens of inmates to Wallens Ridge, Virginia. To this private prison run by 18-year old hillbillies. It was basically state-sanctioned kidnapping. If I live in Connecticut, and broke the law in Connecticut, then I should be incarcerated *in Connecticut*. They shouldn't be allowed to say, "Pack your shit. You're going to fucking Wallens Ridge, Virginia!" But they did. Until everyone threatened to sue, you know, so they ended up sending Mike directly to a federal prison in Lewisburg, Pennsylvania.

I thought, when they popped my door in Cheshire, that I might be headed to the feds right then, too. But no. I was transferred to a different Connecticut state prison. Osborn Correctional Institution. A pretty similar facility to Cheshire, but medium security, you know what I mean? So it was *slightly* more open. We actually ate in a chow hall. Had more time in the yard. More chances to find a job.

During intake, you met with a counselor. To discuss where you might want to work. Right away, I was placed down in industries. Those were really cool jobs to have! You made a decent amount of money and often had freedom to move throughout the prison. There were hundreds of guys that worked in industries. In textiles. In the prison laundry. The print shop. Tech support. Repairs. Plumbing.

I started in the print shop. Where they made all of the business cards and letterhead for the Connecticut State Legislature. At first, I worked in the back room. Packaging shit. And then I was promoted to clerk. Dollar an hour. Six hours a day. That was top pay! And it was super easy. When an order came in, I'd pass it on to the guys in the back. They'd package the product, and I'd make sure it was ready for shipping. No, I never did any printing. Most of the day, I just sat at the computer and played *Age of Empires.*

Eventually, I moved over to the prison laundry. Here's how laundry worked at Osborn. You'd drop your bag of dirty clothes into these wooden boxes-on-wheels that were rolled down to industries. Where your clothes were washed and dried, but left in the bag the whole time. So when they came out, they weren't even really that clean. However... you could pay someone who worked in the laundry, like me, for a "special" service. We'd dump your clothes out, wash and dry them separately, fold everything up, and put it all back in the bag. That was a pretty good hustle!

And again, when I worked in the prison laundry, my Wildman nature would sometimes come out. There was this long ramp, probably 100 yards, which lead from the upper level of the prison down to the industries. So I'd let the boxes full of laundry start rolling down the ramp. And then use my upper body to pull myself on top of the cart. And then ride the cart down the ramp! I bet that I was the only inmate in the fucking history of Osborn to ever do that.

There was this dude, Damien, who worked with me in the prison laundry. We would bring the carts down together. Usually like four at a time. Because you have to roll them down slow. But, one day, Damien was being a dick, and he was like, "C'mon. Let's just bring them all." So we tried to roll like eight carts at once, and they were way too heavy to control. We had to let go, you know, and they all went flying down the ramp by themselves. At the bottom, there were these glass doors. On top of a makeshift cinder block wall. And the carts completely tore the doors off! Destroyed the whole fucking wall!

So we had to go back to the laundry and say, "Hey, um, some carts got away from us. And we, uh, broke the jail."

*

The guy that I worked for in the prison laundry pulled some strings. And got me moved to the H Block on the top tier. At Osborn, there was a bottom tier, a middle tier, and a top tier. And the top tier was all single cells in a small hallway. You even got a key, so you could lock and unlock your room by yourself. Those rooms also had windows *that you could open*. Fresh fucking air coming in and out!

When you lived in H Block, the job paid very little, but it was pretty cool. We cleaned the jail in the middle of the night. A small crew of us. Swept and mopped all of the hallways. It was always so quiet. And we'd be so sleepy. The shift lasted only a few hours, and then we'd go back to our cells early in the morning. Try to sleep a little more. Most of the time, though, I'd just stay up all night. So my sleep schedule was all fucked up, but it was worth it for the single cell.

I did so much art when I was in that space. Jeff Green came to Osborn, too, and I continued in the prison art program. I remember smuggling this big roll of canvas back to my room. Cutting the canvas into strips. Hanging them on the wall. I would make these giant paintings. And then hang another piece of canvas over them. When I wanted to paint, you know, I would roll up the outer canvas. And then roll it back down when I was finished. So the COs wouldn't notice when they walked by.

The COs were usually cool. But sometimes, you ran into a scumbag. There had been incidents, you know, not in Connecticut, but in a prison *somewhere*. A prisoner made a sculpture that looked like a gun. And then tried to escape with it. So they made these blanket policies where we weren't allowed to make anything "sculptural." And I had sculpted this really fine bird. From a block of soap. And some fucking CO came through during a shakedown. Took my art supplies. Smashed my bird on the ground.

How long does it take to sculpt a bird out of soap? Haha. I don't know. Time doesn't really matter in prison. I made tons of weird sculptures from soap. And then, later, I started making these elaborate multi-media pieces from different kinds of smuggled materials. Soap and acrylic paint, you know, rolled up fucking magazine pages. Pieces of cardboard. I'd build these wiry looking things from old paper towels. Twist them real tight. And stick them together with floor wax.

In the prison art program, I also became friends with a guy named Dennis. He had been at Osborn for 15 years already and was the prison's longtime librarian. He was also a vicious bass player in the prison band. So I was like,

"C'mon, Dennis. Let me in the band." And he was like, "What do you play?" I was like, "I'm a singer." And he was like, "Oh yeah?" I was like, "I'm not a very good singer. But I sing!" And he was like, "Alright."

Band was fun. We practiced in the same room where they had GED classes. We'd jam and write songs, you know, but never got to play them for anyone. Until, one day, while we were setting up, a teacher came over. He said, "Hey, I have a group of students getting their GEDs, and we're having a graduation. I know that some of you are artists. Can someone write a big fancy 'congratulations' on the chalkboard?" I immediately volunteered: "Okay! But... you have to let my band play the graduation."

So, after looking up how to spell "congratulations," and then writing "congratulations" on the chalkboard, we started joking around: "Wow! Our first gig! We get to play live for a bunch of convicts! Getting their fucking GED in prison! Congratulations asshole!" And then we wrote a song called "Congratulations Asshole." I actually wrote the lyrics. It starts like this: "Congratulations asshole / You finally made your way / To being a nowhere hero."

Pretty good, right?

*

"Blackman, pack your shit!" I had put in almost nine years in state. So when they popped my door, you know, I knew it was time.

The transition to the feds takes a while. They first sent me to the Metropolitan Correctional Center in Manhattan. The place where Epstein killed himself, you know, supposedly. It's like a transfer station in the middle of the city. So you're up on like the 10th floor of this high-rise building. And it was cool. The rec yard was a little outdoor area enclosed with a razor wire fence. So when you were out there shooting hoops, you could see the Statue of Liberty.

There were tons of prisoners there, but you hardly ever saw anyone. The place was sprawling. Huge. But cordoned off, so you only saw whoever was in your cell block. The only person I remember is my giant Russian cellmate. He had "FUCK RATS" written on his shower shoes. And every night, all night, he would yell, "Fuck! Rats! Fuck! Rats!" He claimed, you know, that somebody had ratted on him, but I had my suspicions.

By the time they put me on a plane from New York City to Lewisburg, Pennsylvania, there were only a little more than two years left on my sentence. The plane was full of federal prisoners. I remember, three seats on each side. All the way back. Dudes with their arms crossed and chained to their waist. We were belly-chained together. With shackles on our feet. So you had to walk – dut dut dut dut – doing "The Shackle Shuffle." We get off the plane somewhere in Pennsylvania. And then were herded onto a bus.

Lewisburg Penitentiary. Think *Shawshank Redemption*. That's what it looked like. That's what it felt like. The 20-foot concrete walls all the way around. The guards up in the towers. With their guns. Looking down over the prison yard. And it had that old-school style, you know, with the prison bars. You walk down the hallways, cell after cell after cell, federal prisoners on display.

At Lewisburg, I was finally reunited with my brother Mike. I remember hugging out on the rec yard. His hair was longer. And he had grown this big biker beard. Gotten more tattoos. Some Celtic and Odinist symbols. Because of the tattoos, you know, they originally classified my brother as a white supremacist, and he had spent significant time in a gang unit. Which is hilarious! Because he was always such a homeboy. In jail, he did generally gravitate towards the white boys, but he also hang around with some MS-13 dudes. That's how he got drugs. Cheap heroin. Tobacco.

By this time, cigarettes weren't allowed in prison. But the hillbilly COs always had a big wad of chew in their mouths. They'd spit that disgusting shit into like empty Pepsi bottles. So guys would dig through the trashcans, find the bottles, and collect the spent chew. And then dry it out, you know, resell it as smoking tobacco. My brother loved that shit. Guys who love cigarettes, man, they *love* cigarettes.

Although when I arrived at Lewisburg, Mike was involved in a rehab program for drug and alcohol abuse. And I joined for a little while, too. You received an extra week of "good time" for every three months of being in the program. In the federal prison system, if you're good for a week, then you accrue one day of "good time." That lessens your sentence by a day. And then, if you're bad, they can punish you by taking away "good time."

The rehab program was run by some shithead doctor. Like so many of these people, you know, who worked in the prison system, they claim to be there to help you. But this dude kicked me out of the program. For stealing pencils. Yeah, I took a handful of No. 2 pencils from a drawer. And they caught it on camera. Fuck you.

*

Lewisburg was wide open, you know what I mean? After they opened your door early in the morning, you were just out *all day*. Mostly free, you know, to do whatever.

That said, Lewisburg was also the Wild West. A scary, scary place. If you weren't part of a gang, if you weren't a rat or a child molester, then nobody really messed with you. But... *if you were*, then it could get ugly. Like this one guy from New Hampshire. He was convicted of sexual misconduct with minors he had picked up on the internet. And when he got to Lewisburg, he refused to "check in." I remember him stretching out in the rec yard. Doing karate moves and shit. Trying to look tough. But they just fucking picked him up. And dropped him on his head. Left him convulsing on the concrete.

By "they," I mean the New Hampshire people. That's the way it worked in the feds. There was a real cliquishness. As a community, it was your responsibility to deal with people from your area. So if you're from New York, then the inmates from New York are supposed to deal with you. And there were prisoners from all over the Northeast. As well as some gang members from L.A. who had been displaced to the East Coast. And a lot of D.C. guys. Because D.C. is just a district, you know, so they don't even have state prisons.

Mike and I got lumped in with the New Yorkers. But, yeah, we were finally together in the feds. We even became cellies! And, right away, we set up shop. In prison, separately, we had both learned to tattoo. I had a celly in Cheshire who showed me the ropes. Some different techniques. How to build a gun. From a beard trimmer and a couple of pen tubes. In the feds, too, the COs were unscrupulous, so you could get stuff smuggled in. Tattoo ink. Guitar strings. You pull off the outside part, and underneath, there's a thin wire that can be used to make tattoo needles.

It was a good hustle. If you learned to tattoo halfway decent, then you could get paid. I remember, this one white dude. We tattooed a pistol *on the side of his head*. We also did a tattoo on a guy from the block named Jason. This dude. He was like this big tough D.C. gang member. When it came to getting tattooed, though, he was such a pussy! He wanted the Jason hockey mask tattooed on his side. But then, every couple of minutes, he would scream, "Yo! Stop stop stop! I need to take a break!"

I also remember doing a tattoo on this guy: Skinny Pimp. This one was funny to me. Not because of the tattoo. I don't even remember what it was. But because, before my time at Lewisburg, he and my brother had gotten into a big beef. Where they were like stabbing each other with pens and shit. That all got squashed, I guess, and now they were like friends. Mike was always getting into beefs. Running up debts. Owing people stamps.

Stamps were like currency in the feds. I remember somebody paying me five books of stamps to play for their basketball team. One game, there was a crowd of people watching from the bleachers. And the scorekeeper kept making fun of me: "Look at that dude! He runs up the court like a fucking robot!" There was a play where a guy stole the ball and thought he had a free layup. But I sprinted back, jumped up, and blocked the shot! Highlight style! Off the backboard! And then did the robot dance in the middle of the court. So for the rest of my time in the feds, everyone called me Robot.

There was an MS-13 guy who played basketball. They called him Seven because he was seven feet tall. One morning, I was dumping my tray in the chow hall. And Seven walked up to me: "Yo, Robot. Tell your fucking brother. Stop trying to pass those phony books." My brother had bought some drugs, or paid some debt, with fake stamps. You can imagine, after they've been passed around as currency, stamps start to look pretty beat. So guys would scam. Cut up little pieces of paper. Put them in between stamps. Try to pass them off as full books.

So I went back to the cell, and my brother was sleeping. I was like, "Mike, wake up. Seven wants to know why you gave him some bogus stamps." And he was like, "What? Oh. I don't know. Somebody gave them to me." And then he'd like, call Sandra, cry, and beg for money. And I would just get so frustrated. Because these guys are gang members! You could get killed over any stupid shit. Or, if someone comes after you violently, then you might have to defend yourself. And end up getting more time.

The whole time, even so close to the end, I was always wondering, "Will I ever make it out of here?"

*

On our block, there was this big white guy with a big white beard. For obvious reasons, everyone called him Santa.

Around Christmastime, Santa got a new celly. And, pretty quickly, Santa's new celly got sick of Santa... masturbating in the cell. So, one day, when Santa was coming out of the shower, his celly stabbed the shit out of him. By the time the medics arrived, Santa's guts were all over the floor. I remember being sick to my stomach. Because my brother and a couple of other dudes were laughing, you know, "Haha. That's fucked up. He killed Santa on Christmas." After years of being in a place like Lewisburg, you just become numb to the violence. It's almost like entertainment.

This was near the very end of my sentence. I had probably been at the feds two years and change. A few months in county, five years in Cheshire, four in Osborn, and some time in Manhattan. And then, yeah, Mike and I left Lewisburg together. Not before I had a little trouble getting my "good time" straightened out. I don't know why, but they had scheduled my brother to leave three months ahead of me. I had to have Sandra, and a lawyer, write a bunch of letters to the prison.

So we fought, for quite a while, until they finally recalculated my "good time." And here's how I found out. This piece-of-shit counselor who was in charge of my case. He came up to me in the chow hall: "I don't know who you cried to, Killion. But it must have been the right person. You're going home next week." Like I was being a crybaby, you know, because I wanted to leave that fucking hellhole *when I was supposed to.*

Being that close to leaving. It was such an awesome, awesome, feeling. But, after you hear that you're going home, you don't want to talk too much about it. There are guys, you know, they got "letters." That means a life sentence. They don't have a number for how much time they're doing. Only letters. And might not give a fuck. Somebody might start a fight with you. Just because. So, for that week, as much as possible, I kept that shit to myself.

And then. A few nights before we were set to get on the bus, the dudes in the cell *right fucking next to us* tried to kill each other. With sardine can lids. Imagine having a small razor and your opponent has a small razor. And you're both locked in a space the size of a bathroom. And you just start slashing. Cutting each other and cutting each other and cutting each other. Until one of the guys finally tapped out and was screaming for a CO. And, all of a sudden, the other guy's hands were *in our cell*. Holding the knives. He was like, "Yo, Mike. Take these."

I looked at my brother. He was looking at me. And then... Mike grabbed the knives. It was a split decision. If he didn't take them, I guess, then it might have come back on us somehow. But, now, if we were caught with them, it would be aiding and abetting. Contraband in your cell. We were going to lose "good time." We were going to be sent to seg. And we definitely weren't going home in a few days. So Mike threw those things in the toilet and started flushing like crazy.

The COs came rushing in. Took the two guys away on stretchers. And then, immediately, put us in the shower. Everyone on the block. We had to strip. Kneel. Handcuffed behind our backs. So, you know, a few days before I'm supposed to go home, I'm in handcuffs. Kneeling in the shower. While COs rip apart my cell. Looking to find some bloody fucking sardine can lids. Luckily, the plumbing system worked! Nobody found shit. But Lewisburg was Lewisburg, man. Right up until the last second.

We were being released to a halfway house in Albany, New York. They popped our cell in the morning. Took us down to the bullpen. Briefly. Did a little paperwork. Gave us some gate money and bus tickets. And then... that's it. We just walked out the front gates. Down the road to the bus stop. When they let you out the door, though, you're still a ward of the feds. You're not free to roam around as you please. They know what time the bus is supposed to arrive in Albany. They know what time you're supposed to check in at the halfway house. You're not allowed to deviate from that course *at all*.

But we were such assholes. We got off of the bus at Penn Station. Mike immediately bought a pack of cigarettes. And then Sandra picked us up, and we drove to some lake north of the city. Had a picnic lunch on the beach. And then I went swimming.

FREEDOM
2007-2020

Robert died while I was in prison. Lung cancer. After he passed, Sandra took his pension, and the life insurance money, and moved to Granville, New York. She found an old farmhouse in the middle of nowhere. That's why I'm here. When they release you from the federal prison system, you need an approved family member near a federal halfway house. And the closest one to Granville was in Albany.

Mike and I arrived at the halfway house in September of 2007. The emotions were pretty intense. Because you go from being locked in Lewisburg Penitentiary, this insane fucking place, to being out in the world. Literally overnight. At first, it's pure joy, you know what I mean? The weight of everyday life hasn't fallen down on you yet. You're just so excited *to be free.*

In Albany, in the fall, they hold an event called LarkFest. It's this huge fucking party on Lark Street. I remember walking around and seeing a stage set up. And then being like, "Holy shit! That's Tom Morello!" The guitarist for Rage. And AudioSlave. He was there with a side project called the Night Watchman. So I watched his set. And afterwards, everybody milling about, I reached over the barricade, grabbed the hot mic, and screamed: "Freeeeedommmmm!" The crowd went crazy! A bouncer tried to rip the mic away, but I just kept screaming: "Freedom! Freedom! Freedom!"

In retrospect, I look back and laugh. At what a reckless asshole I was. Like you weren't allowed to sleep with anyone in the halfway house. But… it's coed. And I'd been in prison for 12 years. And that woman over there is giving me I-want-to-fuck-you eyes. Her name was Angela. Her husband was a big time crack dealer, and she got caught up in the mess. Only served a couple of years, you know, and now she was in a halfway house. Hooking up with me. Doing LSD.

There was a guy at the halfway house. A friend of mine from Lewisburg. This kid had made bank. Selling pot and ecstasy and shit at Grateful Dead concerts. You know the whole Dead Head community that follows the Dead all over the country? Well, within that movement – I swear to God – is a bunch of gangsters. Like straight up organized crime. It probably started with the Hells Angels. They used to work security at shows back in the day. But then saw an opportunity. To make a ton of money selling drugs.

So when we realized that my friend was like *connected*, and had gone right back to doing his thing, hustling bud, we were like, "O-kay! What's up?" And this dude supplied us with some pretty good drugs. I mean, you can't smoke pot in the halfway house. Because they drug test you. But… there's no drug test for LSD. At least, there wasn't then, so we'd be tripping our asses off. On the regular.

If you fuck up at the halfway house, then they can still put you back behind bars. So, yeah, I was playing it fast and loose right away. You weren't allowed to have sex. Check. You weren't allowed to do drugs. Check. You weren't allowed to have a cellphone. But I bought one, you know, immediately, as soon as Angela was released from the halfway house. We had to figure out how to see each other!

Although Angela and I also both happened to work at the same place, so we'd sometimes sneak away from the job. That's the first thing that you have to do. If you don't get a job within a certain amount time, then they'll ship you right back to prison. There were specifics places, you know, that had contracts to hire residents of the halfway house. A linen service. A machine shop. I went to work at this big Italian restaurant. As a dishwasher.

To get to work by bus, it took close to 90 minutes. That's how long they'd give me, you know, from when I signed out of the halfway house. But I borrowed some money from Sandra to buy a bike. And then it only took 40 minutes. They'd still allow me the whole 90 minutes though. So I would just take... my... time. It was an amazing feeling. Here I was, after being incarcerated for 12 years, cruising around, aimlessly, on my bike.

That winter, too, I would go snowboarding after work. Lincoln Park was two blocks away from the halfway house. It's like the biggest sledding spot in the Capital District. So, the day after the first snow, I went and bought a cheap knockoff brand board. And walked over to the park. In my work clothes. Sneakers and a leather jacket. I built an enormous jump. And then just started, you know, hitting jumps. If you can believe it, an *Albany Times Union* reporter was there, and he came over to take my picture. I have that picture hanging up at my store. Next to the one of me from 1993.

I have another picture from that day, too. Of some kid asking for my autograph. He saw me hitting jumps and thought it was so spectacular. I was like, "Okay, kid. I'll give you my autograph! But you should know. I'm not anybody."

*

I'm not proud of this, but I wasn't even very attracted to Krystal. Didn't even really like her. She was just someone who worked at the restaurant. That's it.

And when Krystal got pregnant, I'd only been home for a few months. I didn't want to have a baby! No way. Not *with her*. I told her: "This isn't what I want for my life right now." She wasn't trying to hear that. She was adamant, you know, "I'm having this kid anyway." Listen, man. I don't want there to be a whole section of the book where I trash Krystal. But... uh... we don't agree on a lot of things. Alright. I won't say anything else about that.

Krystal and I moved in together. I was supposed to do six months at the halfway house, but they let me leave a few months early. A ward of the federal prison system. On "supervised release." Krystal knew a landlord in Rensselaer, so that's where we ended up. And my daughter was born a few months later. Dangerously premature. The doctor turned to me and said: "Well, the good news is, she has a 50/50 chance of survival." I was like, "Holy shit! That's the good news????"

She was intubated in a NICU unit for a long fucking time. But once my daughter came home, she was strong and healthy. And... amazing! When you have your own child, this little peanut, with these fat cheeks, yeah, you fall in love pretty quickly. Her name is Reilley. I wanted to call her Dani, of course, but Krystal had other ideas. She liked the name Reilley. It's Irish or something. I don't know.

Once the euphoria wore off, it was a totally miserable situation. I slept on the couch every night and woke up early to go to work. And if I wasn't working, then I had to watch Reilley. Feed her. Change her diapers. All of that stuff. I didn't want to be doing it. I wasn't great at it. I was fucking resentful of Krystal the whole time. We were never happy together. Even before Reilley was born, you know, but then it just got worse and worse.

I spent a year and a half trying to do the right thing. At a certain point, though, enough was enough. I couldn't live with Krystal anymore. I still wanted to be around to help take care of my daughter, though, so I literally moved into an apartment *next door*. My buddy Chris lived there. He was a snowboarder, too, and we were fast friends. And had been hanging out, partying, and having fun.

On probation, however, having fun can sometimes come back to bite you in the ass. The probation period lasts for five years, and you have to check in every night.

To see if you have to give a urine sample the next day. It was like an automated system. You called, entered in your number, and it said, "You do *not* have to report for urine analysis in the morning." But, every now and then, randomly, you did.

I remember hanging out next door. This was before we were roommates. Chris had some friends over, and they were all doing coke. So I checked in, and the automated system said that I did not have to report in the morning. I thought, "Cool. I'll hang out and do some drugs with my buddies." I only did one line. But, of course, the next time I checked in, it said that I did have to report. And my urine was dirty. And they made me attend drug counseling. Every Tuesday and Thursday night. For six months.

That wasn't even my worst trouble. I remember, we went to Schenectady for a St. Patrick's Day party. And parked, I guess, somewhere we weren't supposed to. And when we came out of the bar, I saw my buddy's car on the back of a flatbed. I yelled, "Yoooooo!" Ran over, you know, climbed up next to the driver's side window: "We're here now, man. Just put it down." The driver said, "Nope. I'm not putting it down." I was like, "C'mon, dude. I'll give you $50." But he was like, "Sorry. This car is getting towed."

So... I might have gotten into a *slight* altercation. Smacked him around a little bit. And then, all of a sudden, there were cops everywhere. Pulling me off of the truck. Spraying me in the face with mace.

*

I got arrested. For "interfering with a police operation." Luckily, the tow-truck driver didn't press charges, but it was still a violation of my probation. I had to wear an ankle bracelet and be home every night by 9:00 for 90 days. They don't want to send you back to jail. They try not to, you know, but they will. If you get *really* out of line.

Like my brother Mike. In the beginning, he did okay. But then he got a DWI, which is a violation of his probation and also a felony. So he went back to prison. For three months. He came out, and within two weeks, got *another* DWI. And went back in for *another* three months. Came out, again, and then was just defeated, you know what I mean? It was frustrating. Dealing with his bullshit. While trying to deal with my own.

When Mike and I first got out, we both were doing a little side hustle. Tattooing. On the back porch of my apartment. And Mike told me, you know, over the phone, that he didn't want to have that pistol. He had just done a tattoo for some guy who didn't have any money. So the guy gave Mike a pistol. That's what Mike always does. Make excuses. "It's not my fault. This happened and that happened." But things are how they are, man. And Mike got caught with a pistol under the seat of his car.

So, yeah, my brother's back in prison. And he still has a long way to go. His new release date is 2029.

*

At the big Italian restaurant, they promoted me to kitchen care supervisor. I planned the schedule for all of the other dishwashers and made sure that every part of the kitchen was cleaned and maintained. They gave me a salary: $600 a week. It was exciting. Looking back, though, after taxes, that's no money at all. And I was working a ridiculous amount. Like 60 hours a week!

Anyway. I ended up getting fired from that job. Because of this other employee. A friend of mine from the halfway house: a Puerto Rican guy named Louis. He and three waiters, non-halfway house residents, you know, regular civilians, they were running a scam. Stealing gift cards. And the bosses found out. And rather than just reprimand them, or even fire them, the bosses called in the state police to arrest them. It was totally fucking unnecessary. In my personal opinion.

Even worse. One of the civilians tried to place *all* of the blame on my buddy Louis. He tried to be like: "It wasn't us, man. It was only this guy. The Puerto Rican ex-con." I thought that was a scumbag move. So when Louis left me a message that he and this waiter were hanging out at some bar, I went over there. And maybe tried to "influence" the dude to have a "different perspective." Haha. He didn't appreciate my influence, I guess, and told the bosses at the restaurant.

These guys. They think they're like junior mafia or something. Go around in fancy Cadillacs and long black trench coats. So corny. I was working in the kitchen when they called me up to the office. Here he was – the head boss – with some big guido standing next to him. He squinted, "I don't know what your story is, but you're done here." I looked at the big guido, and then back at the head guy, and then started laughing my ass off. I was like, "C'mon. Come. On. You are so fucking corny! I'm a *dishwasher*. What the fuck do I care?"

For a while, after that, I would do odd jobs. Wake up early. Head over to a place in downtown Albany called Labor Ready. They hired day laborers. Sandra had lent me an old Chevy Astro Van that was just sitting around her property in Granville. So, because I had a car, you know, I would always get hired to do something. They'd say, "Hey, Killion! Do you want to work today?" And then add, "Could you possibly drive two other guys with you?"

I did all kinds of shitty gigs. Mostly construction. But I got to ride around in a garbage truck one time. That was pretty fun! I also went to the University of Albany, once, and opened this little café, you know, after their employees had all called out sick. I had no idea what I was doing! Didn't know how to work the register. Didn't know how to make anything on the fucking menu. When students tried to order, I'd be like, "Uh. How about an egg sandwich?"

But then, one day, they sent me out to this construction site to do some work for a subcontractor. They were building shitty condos and just needed some extra hands. Here I was, you know, almost 40 years old, doing hard labor. Carrying fucking heavy-ass fire doors. Although I met some of the carpenters. Who introduced me to the owner of the company. I looked at him straight: "Yo! I need a job. Teach me how to do some of this stuff. Hire me on full-time."

I never really knew that much about carpentry. So the other carpenters, mostly good dudes, would share with me what they knew. It's not nearly as complicated as people might think. To do high-end carpentry, yeah, you need to have some skill and experience. But the basic stuff? It's a little bit of math and a little bit of paying attention. Learning how to read a tape measure. That's probably the most important thing.

The type of carpentry that we were doing is called "shit n' get." That means: it doesn't have to be perfect. Just take your low-end materials, you know, fucking particle board. Put it on and move along. Fast, fast, fast. Because that's how you make your money. We did miles and miles of baseboard. Apartment after apartment. Think about a building that has six units upstairs and six units downstairs. Twelve total. All need baseboard. All need crown molding. All need kitchen cabinets.

So I didn't have to be the best carpenter in the world. And... I'm still not. I've always thought of myself more as an artist, you know what I mean?

*

My boss: Dick. I worked at his company for almost five years. By the time I left, I had made my way up to being the foreman. The previous foreman was a talented carpenter, but a vicious alcoholic. Would get so wasted, you know, that he couldn't even wake up in time to be on the job site.

At this point in my life, I had quit drinking. I had quit everything. I was super sober. I remember sitting on my porch, smoking a cigarette, drinking a beer *and* a mixed drink, after having smoked weed *and* eaten some mushrooms. The next day, you know, I was like, "Nah. Enough of this. I'm done." It was a point of pride. And the more Dick moved me up, the more I wanted to just really focus on my job. There were way better carpenters on that crew, but Dick made me foreman. Because he thought that I was responsible.

On the other hand, Dick himself was a despicable person. Misogynist. Crass. Dishonest. Cut corners. We did doors and trim, you know, and had to bid against other companies for jobs. So Dick would bid really low. And then send me random guys that he found in *The Schenectady Gazette*. These weren't professional carpenters. Sometimes, he'd even bring in his 16-year old son to help me finish a project.

It was always such a shitshow. Like we were on this $500,000,000 job. A *huge* site. Where we had 20 units to remodel. And then build ten more brand new units. Not just us. We were only one of the subcontractors. There were framing subcontractors. Roofing subcontractors. Plumbing subcontractors. And this big company that hired everyone: BBL. Dick had me running a crew of six guys, but these guys were nowhere near good enough to meet BBL's standards. Never mind keep up with the timeline.

So Dick brought in another sub. These Brazilians. Like four dudes. Who were way better than any of the carpenters that he normally hired. They would show up every day and absolutely kill it. And when they finished, the head BBL guy said to me: "Danny, we're done. Tell Dick to pay these guys." But Dick didn't want to give them the money. So he'd be on the phone with me: "Danny, walk around the building and find things that are wrong. Make stuff up." And I thought to myself: "Nah. That's bullshit.

I'm not doing that." These guys did their job. Fucking saved your ass. Pay up!

I stuck it out with Dick. For the job security. You need to keep a job when you're on probation. Plus, the pay was decent. Although, as soon as I had enough money to invest, I also started dealing weed. It just happened organically. That friend of mine who I reconnected with at the halfway house. The Dead Head. He was just a really good source. Could get me a good price for a good product.

To start, you bought a pound of weed. At $80-100 an ounce. For decent weed, you could sell an ounce for $250 and make a solid profit. Or... you could sell half ounces, quarters, even eighths. And if you took an $80 ounce and sold each eighth for $40, then you could make tons of money. It's more hand-to-hand that way, but it's not very hard to find customers. I mean, uh, a lot of people smoke weed! Half the fucking planet smokes weed! And the dudes that worked construction, they all smoked weed!

My weed operation got bigger when I reconnected with another friend from prison. Remember Damien? He worked with me in the prison laundry. Well, he was still in Connecticut. And we had remained friends, you know, had a lot in common. We were both biracial. White mothers, Black fathers. We were both bank robbers. Damien was a bad bank robber, though. Only robbed one bank and got caught. No mask. Left the gun in the bushes *with his fingerprints still on it*. Amateur moves. C'mon, dude. He could sure fucking ship some weed though!

And happened to have a source. Some guy out west. And then Damien himself moved out to Sacramento. So then we were moving like 15 pounds per month, you know, from the west to the east. Putting it into circulation. Five pounds at a time. That's an easier deal. One shot. I process the product, someone shows up to my place, buys a five-pack, and we make $900 a pound. And Damien trusted me. He'd send me weed, I'd flip it over, and then hold onto the money. Until he and his guy came east, every now and then, to pick up their cut in person.

There were ups and downs, too. Lost packages. Lost money. Quiet times. But we got ahead more often than not. Made more selling weed than I did working construction. The construction, though, was *consistent*. At the end of my construction career, I was taking home $800 a week. Which is not terrible. You can pay your bills on that. And there are never losses in construction. But... it's your whole life! Fifty hours a week. When I could make $1000 in one deal selling weed.

One time, I remember, their cut was $52,000. So I was sitting at my coffee table trying to count out the $52,000 in cash. And my roommate came walking through the room. And he looked at all of the money on the coffee table. Just shook his head, you know, and went into the bathroom.

*

I had stopped down by the riverfront after work. There was a nice spot near my apartment in Rensselaer. Not even a mile away. This little park with picnic tables. You could see all of Albany right across the river.

So, that day, I was just sitting there, chilling, but then I saw *something*. An old stump. It had a giant rock embedded in the center. There were wrinkles in the wood where it grew up around the rock. And then, on top, two weird-looking arms. Super smooth from being in the river for so long. Since then, I've found tons of cool shit by the river, but nothing exactly like that stump. And that's when I started, you know, walking the river and collecting driftwood to make art.

And then I started hanging out with some people from the Albany art scene. I had answered an ad on Craigslist. This place called Silver Fox Salvage was looking for part-time help. It was a store in the warehouse district downtown. The owners were doing all kinds of interesting work with reclaimed material. They also rented out sections of their warehouse space to local artists. So I worked there for a little while. Built stuff. Hung chandeliers. Made deliveries. Whatever they needed.

There was another guy who worked there part-time: Martin Dodge. He was this really dynamic florist. Had his own business called Drops of Jupiter. I showed him some of my driftwood pieces, and he was like, "Cool, man. We should do a collaboration." So we did an installation for a gallery opening. In the hallway leading into the gallery, you know, I built these huge driftwood structures, and Martin decked everything out with flowers. It was really wild. To see how amazed the other artists were by something that, I thought, was pretty simple to achieve.

Martin and I collaborated once again at New York in Bloom. It was an annual Albany flower show inside of the New York State Museum. A whole bunch of florists would participate. Some just did bouquets. Some would do these huge elaborate displays. They would charge tickets, you know, and all of the money went to local charities. So I worked on displays with Martin, a few years in a row, and began to build some momentum. Towards having a business of my own.

That's when I met Kate. My all-the-way crazy ex, you know, girlfriend and business partner. I was at Home Depot, and she was checking me out. As in, *she was the checkout girl*. Very attractive. Brunette. Green eyes. Great figure. I flirted with her a little bit, and she was responsive. And then she called me. At the time, Kate was also bizarrely into making things with driftwood. So we were vibing on that level. Creatively.

Shit got messy right away. When Kate came into the picture, Krystal was, uh, not happy. Like I was playing poker with a bunch of my buddies, and Kate was over at the house. And Krystal stormed into the apartment when Kate was in the bathroom. She fucking kicked the bathroom door open: "Get out of here, bitch!" And Kate was just sitting there, peeing, you know, like: "What the fuck is happening right now?" Oh my god. I'm a little embarrassed of that story. It's so trashy!

It was always a little tense. Because Krystal hated Kate. And Kate actually moved into that apartment when my roommate Chris moved out. And then Kate's friend Charlotte needed a place to stay, so she moved in, too. For a while there, it was me, Kate, and her friend Charlotte. I was working full-time construction, moving up in the company, on my way to being foreman. This was when I just decided, you know, to get sober. My job was important to me, you know what I mean?

So, one night, I was trying to go to bed, and Kate and Charlotte were up making noise. And I came out of my bedroom: "Hey, I have to be up at 5:00 in the morning. Could you guys keep it down?" Kate was so offended that, the next morning, she texted: "I'm moving out. And Charlotte's moving out with me." I responded, "It's not that big of a deal. We could probably work this out." But she was like, "Nope. We're breaking up."

And then I was mad, you know, the whole day. When I got home from work, however, Kate was still there: "Oh, I was just kidding! I don't really want to break up. I just didn't like that you were chastising me, so I wanted to teach you a lesson." Oh yeah? Here's the problem. Now you're *definitely* moving out! Because I'm a grown-ass man. And no crazy chick is going to teach me a fucking lesson. By playing games with my heart.

That's what I said to her. And then kicked them both out of my house! I was like, "Pack. Your. Shit."

*

Eventually, it got ugly enough living next door to Krystal that I moved. To an apartment in Troy. A little closer to my construction job. But then Kate moved into an apartment like two blocks away from me. And we would run into each other all of the time. And then we started talking again. And hanging out. And dating. On and off, you know, back and forth. For years.

One Sunday morning, after I moved to Troy, I was driving around. I had my daughter Reilley with me. When she was younger, you know, I would take her on the weekends. So we're in the car together and passed this church. There was a woman, out front, hanging pieces of paper along an iron fence. It looked like some kind of art project. So I pulled over: "Hey, what's going on here?" And she explained to me what she was doing. And then she explained what the place all was about.

The Contemporary Art Center of Troy. The CAC. Henry Burden – of the old Burden Iron Works – had built this huge church up on the hill. Well, some local artists had saved the church. Turned the rectory into these little campy lofts. And founded an artist residency. Artists would come from all over the world, you know, stay for a few weeks, make art, and do shows. I thought, "Whoa. I want to be involved with this."

So I reached out to Hezzie Phillips, the woman who ran the organization, and she actually had an opening for a position as caretaker. You received a little bit of studio space in exchange for like 15 hours a week. I remember being really nervous when I applied. Fingers crossed, you know, and I got the gig. The place was falling apart, so they had plenty of work for me. Maintenance. Walls. Flooring. Plumbing. Some stuff – like running gas line – I was capable of doing, but they probably should have hired a fucking professional. You know how it is with artists. Always broke!

I did meet tons of interesting people at the CAC. Like I now have Facebook friends from Australia. And Japan. And *everywhere*. They would hold these dinners. The volunteers, and residents, and board members would come. And we'd go around, you know, everybody would say who they were, where they came from, what particular media they worked in, what they were currently working on.

I remember, once, I brought Kate to a CAC dinner, and she got really obnoxiously drunk. And as we were going around, Kate interrupted, "This is cool. Let's do fetishes." And then yelled out: "Danny has a foot fetish!" I was fucking mortified. And Kate couldn't understand why. I was like, "You don't see how that's fucked up? Blurting out in front of 20 people, some of them strangers, some of them *my employers*, that I have a foot fetish!" And she was like, "No. I don't." So I just shook my head, you know, "Okay."

Overall, I had a great experience at the CAC, although it was occasionally frustrating. The organizers were super idealistic, but not, let's say, pragmatic. When it came to their volunteers and work-exchange people, their expectations were outrageous. So I didn't stay very long. However, while I was there, I did begin to develop my craft. That's where I started, you know, making the lamps and other pieces of furniture. In the style that we sell in our store today.

Back then, I worked out at this gym in Troy called Maximum Fitness. This wasn't like some highfalutin look-at-me-I'm-so-pretty kind of Planet Fitness gym. No. It was just like working-class guys with their boots still on. Located in this old factory. Four stories tall. So after I'd work out, I'd roam around the building. In the basement, there was a sprinkler company. On the first floor, a ceramics supplier. On the second floor, my gym. But the third and fourth floors were… totally empty.

I actually called a realtor and asked about the building. They said, "Well, if you know the place, just go talk to the landlord." So I went down into the basement and found the guy. This 89-year old dude. A sprinkler installer. Still working. Crushed a case of Budweiser every day. His grandson also worked with him on the sprinkler business. And they were always frantic, you know, because the building was a pain-in-the-ass to maintain. But for only $500 a month, they rented me the whole 4th floor. Twenty-five foot ceilings. You could fit half of downtown Troy in that space!

I got so much production done there. Driftwood work. Metal sculptures. Big furniture. Giant installations. Kate would come hang around the studio, and I'd show her how to use some of the tools. And then she started making cool stuff, too. We were doing shows. Getting good response. And her work was doing well. And my work was doing well. And we were selling a lot, you know, through other stores in town.

When they decided to turn that whole building into condos, Kate and I finally pulled the trigger. On starting our own company. I quit working construction, and we found a place in downtown Troy. A storefront with a basement workshop. And then I'd either work in my backyard, in the workshop, or out on the sidewalk, in front of our store. Weathered Wood.

*

A funny story just came to mind.

This kid named Sean had worked as an apprentice on my construction site. He sold a little bit of weed for me, too. But then, you know, he was laid off from the company. And then just bounced. Totally disappeared. Stopped answering his phone. Still owing me a few hundred dollars. And that was that. Until... I heard about a show coming up at the fairgrounds in Altamont, New York. A metal festival. The band Mudvayne was in the lineup, and I fucking knew Sean would be there.

So I went to the show with Kate. We're walking around, and – sure enough – she was like, "Holy shit! Is that him over there?" I ran over. Tapped him on the shoulder. When Sean turned around, man, he almost shit his pants. I was laughing, "Dude, I'm not going to beat you up! But here's the deal. To pay off the debt, you have to help me out on a project." So, early on, when we started the store, Sean helped me build these little racks to organize driftwood in my basement workshop.

Pretty shortly after that, I got out of the weed game. Somebody out west, *somebody*, mailed four pounds of marijuana to the store. How would I know where the marijuana came from? I have no idea. But whoever mailed it, mailed it through the United States Post Office. Instead of FedEx or UPS which they're supposed to use. And a United States Postal Service federal agent caught the weed. Brought the weed to my store. And then promptly arrested me and charged me with possession.

Those charges were fortunately dismissed, but that was beginning of the end. The quality of the weed started to slip. They were trying to cut corners out west, you know, make more money for themselves. It was very frustrating! Like we had a pretty thriving marijuana business. If they had just been willing to keep the quality consistent, and not be so fucking greedy, then I could've had $150,000 in a shoebox under my bed right now.

The end of the end came when Damien – someone who I trusted, who I really considered a friend, even family, you know what I mean? – burned me out of a lot of money. He burned both of us: me and his guy out west. But Damien specifically stole fucking $7,500 *from me*. And now he's living way down in Trinidad. Yeah, man, if I ever see that dude again… he's dead to me. At the very least.

The look on your face. I know what you're thinking: "I'm not sure if I want to hang out with Danny anymore." But this is a real thing in my life. I try to hustle. I try to make a living. It's hard and things are stacked against you. Especially as an ex-con. If I didn't break the law a little bit, bend it, try to get away with shit whenever I can, then I don't think I could ever get ahead. Rich people, they make all of the rules anyway. Rig the whole fucking game.

For example. From the very beginning of our business, we've been making these driftwood lamps. And Kate and

I, you know, we would walk into TJ Maxx and see similar products. But nowhere near as good as what we were making. So I actually called up the TJ Maxx corporate office and spoke with the head merchandiser. We had a pretty good conversation, and then I emailed her a bunch of pictures. She said, "These are amazing. Can you ship us a sample?" We packaged up a few different products and sent them off to headquarters in Framingham, Massachusetts.

And then the head merchandiser called me. She said, "We love your lamps. Can you make a thousand of these a month?" So I was like, "Holy shit. I just hit the big time. I now have my own fucking production company!" We asked for $12 per lamp. But they came back like: "Nah, man. No way. We can buy these from China super cheap. If you'll take $3 apiece, then we have a deal." What the fuck? I was paying $5 apiece just to make them! So that dream was dead in the water. Before it even started.

*

It feels like so long ago. When I moved out of the halfway house, Jeff Green – my old art teacher – actually came to my apartment and brought me art supplies. What an amazing fucking person. We've stayed in touch over the years. And then, one day, he stopped into the store, you know, just passing through. He was still working in the prison art program. That's when I said to him: "Dude, I'm a living example of how beneficial the program is. You should really let me share that with people."

So, immediately, Jeff talked somebody into letting me install two big sculptures in front of the juvenile detention center in downtown Hartford. One was this really crazy old root system that I had found along the river and then mounted on two poles. The other was this four by eight foot board covered in reclaimed and painted electrical cable. Like a giant biomechanical microchip. Jeff told me that he heard somebody walk by it and say, "What. The fuck. Is *that*."

Jeff has also invited me to speak at three different art openings in Connecticut: the annual showing, you know, of work by prisoners in the program. The first time was before a huge audience at this really cool museum. Packed with people as far as I could see. The most recent time was at the Hartford Public Library. Right in the heart of downtown. The mayor of Hartford was there!

In prison, I was always so stoked for the annual show. Most facets of the prison system are just designed to keep you caged and docile. So, especially when you're locked up for a long time, it's very easy to fall into a negative perspective. The prison art program, though, had such a profoundly positive effect on my life. This is what I said to those audiences. The program saved me. Helped me keep connected to who I was. Helped me look forward. And now I'm an artist. Who supports other artists. Who is part of a community. Who has his own small business.

The business became *my own* when Kate and I split. As business partners. We were feuding all of the time. One day, we were in the middle of a big fight. I was working on the sidewalk, and Kate came out: "Hey, somebody wants to buy the stump. Is it for sale?" The original old stump. I had kept it on display in the store. But, that day, I said, "Yeah. Fuck it. I don't care." And sold it for $100. I really regret letting that piece go, you know what I mean? I should have kept it. *Forever*.

We still dated on and off, but Kate started her own store. Which failed pretty quickly. So I let her sell stuff out of – what was now – my store. One night, I was finishing a project for a deadline. Kate showed up wasted. Looking to help. I was like, "No. I don't need your help. Please go." And she freaked out and stabbed me in the genitals with a paintbrush. I called the cops, but they showed up and made *me* leave *my* store. And then she fucking smashed the window of my truck with a brick. And then came up to my apartment to yell at me. And I dragged her back down a flight of stairs. By a fistful of hair.

She still had some of my property. So, days later, I went over to her apartment, knocked on the door, and said, very nicely, "Hey, can I have my TV and my DVD player back?" And… she called the cops. And, once again, they showed up and made me leave. But I still had a spare key for her truck. So… I stole it. Didn't keep it or anything. Nah. I just parked it some other place. A few blocks away.

*

It's been two years since Kate's been completely out of my life. Things are so much chiller now. I have a cordial relationship with Reilley's mother Krystal. My daughter is twelve years old – pretty much how long I've been out of prison – and we see each other all of the time. Go to the movies. Hit the Chinese buffet.

Reilley attends school right here in Troy. She'll come downtown on the bus with her friends. Stop by the store: "Hey, dad! How's it going?" And it's been great, especially recently, because there are so many really cool, strong, progressive women around me. My daughter's been to a Black Lives Matter protest! She's been on a bullhorn, you know, calling out the chant: "No justice! No peace!" She fucking skateboards! And she's good, too. Even better than Rosemarie.

The wonderful Rosemarie. We met on the streets of Troy. I was riding a giant metal spool. It was used to wind up gas line. I found it discarded behind a closed down sushi restaurant on Central Avenue in Albany. Kept it in front of the store for a while. And then I'd ride it, up and down the street, you know, during the farmer's market. I could get that thing going pretty fast, jump on and then jump off, lie down in the street, and let it roll over me. Jump back on from the other side.

She walked by. Super short dyed-blonde hair. That fucking smile. I said, "Do you want to give it a try?" And she said, "Uh. Yep. Definitely." I remember, she just kicked off her shoes and jumped on. I thought, "Who the hell is this girl?" So I found out. Low-key stalked her. She was cutting hair out of this small art gallery called American Grit. I walked in there, all cocky, like the fucking King of Siam: "What's up? You want to go out some time?"

Rosemarie has a different story of when she first saw me. There used to be a storytelling series in Troy, the third Tuesday of every month, called Front Parlor. Just regular people, you know, telling their tales. I went there a few times with my crazy-ass ex. Walked up on stage and rattled off some of my classic bank robbing stories. And, one night, well before we met, Rosemarie happened to be in the audience.

Her energy. She's tiny, you know, but fucking enormous at the same time. A beautiful soul. Kind and loving and sincere. Only *a little bit* crazy. I'm super lucky that she's still with me. We dated for a while, but then it felt too serious, too fast. So I ended things. And she left town soon after. Lived with some other guy out in the suburbs. Almost two years later, she texted me: "Hey, I'm looking to move back to Troy. Do you have any leads on an apartment?" As soon as I got that text message, I knew, I needed Rosemarie back in my life. And I fucking told her so.

That was a weird time. I was buying a house. Feeling a lot of work stress. So we got in a fight, and – like an asshole – I broke up with her again. It wasn't pretty. She was very, very, upset. Immediately, I understood my mistake. Begged her and begged her to *please* give me one more chance. And then she went on a trip, and I took care of her dog Waylon. We texted the whole time. Talked on the phone. And when she got back, I had gotten a tattoo on my chest: "Rose Wildflower Little Spoon Savage, I am forever yours."

She was… surprised. But I told her: "I won't break your heart anymore." And she decided to take me back. This was a year and a half ago. And then I closed on the house. My buddy Brian – a local ceramic artist *and* doctor – owns a bunch of properties in North Troy. He showed me this place.

It's only a few blocks away from the CAC. A little ghetto in spots. The bodega on the corner. There's always like four or five brothers outside. Shooting dice and drinking at 11:00 in the morning. But it's also getting more gentrified. You'll see young white women walking their dogs.

We love it here. Rosemarie and Waylon moved in with me. We'll just come home and be like.... ahhhh. I mean, it's really run down. A friend of ours saw it from the outside and said, "You *live* there?" But we're going to work on it, you know, over the years. Eventually, it'll be like our mansion. And even right now, currently, the way it is, we are both always reflecting upon how much we love having our own place. In this town. Somewhere we've been for a while. Where we know so many cool people.

Troy is our family. As you know, from earlier stories, I don't particularly care for the people who adopted me. So the people in this community who I've chosen to be around, the ones that I like, even the ones that I don't, you know, that's what they are. My family.

DO YOU WANT TO HEAR A CRAZY STORY?

January 2021

Dude. Listen to this bullshit. At the end of August, I received a letter from the fucking Attorney General of the United States. Where he says that I owe the federal government... wait for it... $89,000.

If you have money in a bank, and that bank gets robbed, then you don't lose your money. It's all federally insured, you know, FDIC. But the feds make bank robbers pay them that money back *in restitution*. It's a big scam. Because, number one, when we got busted, they took everything that we had on us, maybe $25,000, and that money never found its way back to the feds. Number two, the banks themselves always lie and overreport how much was actually stolen. Pretty fucked up, right?

You don't have to pay while you're in the joint. As soon as you get home, though, your probation officer will ask, "Are you paying restitution?" The other guy in our crew, Brent, he's still in prison. So when my brother went back, all of the restitution fell on me. I would slow-pay it, $20, $30, $40 at a time. Just so I could say, "Yep. I made a payment." But once I was off probation, I stopped paying it altogether. I figured, "That was twenty-five years ago. They don't really care." Well, *I was wrong*.

It's fucking 2021. I haven't paid restitution for almost ten years! In this letter, they claim that the remaining principal is $39,000, but they've also tacked on $50,000 *in interest*. I can't believe that Uncle Sam has the time and energy to chase me down! Big corporations get away with murder! The Donald has barely paid any income tax since

I was in prison! But, hey, this Dan Killion guy. Let's make him pay.

I had a lawyer-friend take a look at the paperwork they sent. She brought it back to me and said, "Fill it out." It was like ten fucking pages. So I filled out the first page with my name, address, and social security number. The second page asked for my business information and bank account numbers. I was like, "Uh. I'm not giving this to the federal government. No way." My lawyer-friend was like, "You have to." And I said, "But... I don't want to." And she said, "But... you have to." So the forms sat there on my dining room table. Until October.

I did finally fill it all out. We'll see if we can negotiate some sort of payment plan. That's the best I can hope for. My lawyer-friend pleaded with them: "C'mon. This dude is fucking broke. He doesn't have $89,000! Can we set him up to pay something like $50 a month?" Directly, you know, from my bank account. We haven't heard back yet. Whatever happens, I'm pretty much fucked financially. For the rest of my life.

I was someone who was destitute, so I robbed banks. And you sent me to prison. And told me that was restitution. And now you say I still owe $89,000. Including $50,000 in interest. What the fuck? This. Is. Why. I. Robbed. Banks. In the first place!

*

This lawyer-friend, the one helping me sort out the restitution, is also helping with my case against the city of Troy. Her name is Tamara. When she first moved to the neighborhood, we would bump into each other while dog-walking. Stop and chat, you know, and then she started coming by the store. One day, I was telling her about my situation, and she said that she was a defense lawyer. And volunteered to lend a hand, pro bono, in exchange for a nice wood top table.

This isn't the same lawyer-friend who was originally helping me. The woman who owns the restaurant next door to the store, Heidi. *Her wife* Kelly is a corporate lawyer who had volunteered her time back in January. She gave me some early legal advice-assistance, but then didn't do much after that. Not that I'm complaining. You don't look a gift horse in the mouth! And when Tamara entered the picture, Kelly was totally cool with it: "The more, the merrier."

Because of COVID, it wasn't until seven months after the accident that we finally went to court. It's ludicrous. Instead of saying, "Our officer made a mistake. Let's make sure that he knows his mistake. So, next time, he doesn't kill someone. We apologize to the community member. Reimburse him for his vehicle. And politely ask him not to sue us." Instead of saying *that*, you know, they issued me a ticket for "failure to yield to an emergency vehicle." They just won't admit that they were at fault *in any way*.

In court, the city did make an offer. If I plead guilty, then they'd let me plead to a lesser offense. "Parking on pavement." This is a common practice in traffic violations. Most people take the deal. But I told them: "Fuck you. No deal." So... we adjourned for a month. In the meantime, Tamara did a little more research on what our burden would be and what their burden would be. Basically, she said, we had to prove "reckless disregard" on the part of the officer.

We have a video. From a camera attached to a house on the corner of the intersection. And the video *clearly* shows this cop blasting through the red light. He was the only one who had any chance to prevent the accident. When he's coming to the light, he should have slowed down and checked to see that nobody was coming. That's the policy. That's what they're supposed to do. We asked for his dashboard cam, you know, which would show how fast he was going. They said, "File a FOIL request." So we filed a FOIL request. They denied our FOIL request.

If we brought it to trial, then they would have to allow the video and the dashboard cam. How could I possibly be found guilty? Even still, I had a sneaking feeling that I was going to get fucked. That the system would work to protect the municipality at all costs. So, finally, at the strong suggestion *of both* of my lawyer-friends, I plead guilty to "parking on pavement." Paid the $50 fine and moved on.

Last year, before February even rolled around, we had submitted an official request to the city. I wanted them to replace my van. And compensate me for the time that I wasn't able to work. That seemed like a reasonable request, you know, from someone who they almost fucking killed. But I've been calling City Hall all year. I just called a few days ago. On January 11th: the one-year anniversary of my accident. No one called me back. No one ever calls me back.

If this never gets resolved, then we could sue the city in civil court. Or even sue the officer directly. But there's fear, you know, that they know *exactly* who I am. The police chief can say, "Hey, when you see Danny driving around, pull him over." Or: "Hey, go check if Danny is up to snuff on all of his codes." These little ways that they can fuck with you. And they will. They're a gang. Right from the mayor down to the cop who hit me. Governments, I believe, on every level, are corrupt and disgusting.

The deputy mayor is actually an acquaintance of mine. Her name is Monica. I know her from when she used to manage the farmer's market. She actually texted me before Christmas to ask if I wanted to set up an outdoor booth during the Victorian Stroll. It's this annual holiday event downtown. But the space she offered is only a block away from my store. And directly in front of a restaurant that closed down because of COVID. So, if I set up a booth, and make things look festive, then it's free decorating for the city.

She's a politician, you know what I mean? I've sent her texts about my case: "I thought we were friends. Politics are one thing. But I'm a human being. How are you letting this happen?" She never responds, you know, but then she'll text, "Hey Danny. I just sent a friend of mine your info. She's looking for a nice piece to hang on her wall."

*

It's a "hard conversation." That's what I said on Instagram, you know, when I updated the community. In September, when our three-year lease was up, we really considered shutting down Weathered Wood. Our landlord, though, agreed to keep the rent steady, so we signed on for another year. But now we've been talking seriously. About whether or not we can afford to keep the storefront open.

I mean, it has just been such a slow year for retail. From the very beginning. There's usually the Capital District Garden and Flower Show in March. They sell tickets, and the organizers pay the exhibitors. The budget for that show is $4,000, but we usually only spend about $500. And, the last few years, we've done thousands of dollars *more* business through people who saw me there. So, the end of March hits, you know, and – boom! – we bank $5,000-6,000 right away.

That was the first thing to be cancelled. And then the farmer's market. In the summertime, on weekends, we can make enough money to pay the rent. And there have been no weddings this year. With church weddings being less common, and outdoor weddings being more common, I fell into this niche of bringing driftwood arbors directly to the ceremonies, you know, in a field or by the edge of some lake. On average, I charge $300 to rent one of my arbors. Last year, we probably did about 40 weddings. This year, we've only done three. So that's been devastating. Without question.

It's been a little better around the holidays. But January and February, coming up, are the worst months for retail. When will things get back to normal? Frontline workers are getting vaccinated soon. *Maybe* a significant portion of the population will be vaccinated by April. *If*, you know, the numbers go down, and the farmer's market returns, then I'll be kicking myself for leaving this space. On the other hand, if I do spend a lot of money to keep the space open, and then business doesn't come back, then what?

We should be able to make it, at least, until the end of March. The landlord *reluctantly* gave us a three-month 50% reprieve on our rent. He was like, "What about your hair stylist friend? How's *she* doing?" And Rosemarie has been doing okay. She hasn't stopped booking appointments, and her clientele is super happy with the new space. We built this dope little salon, you know, it would be such a shame to shut it down.

*

Maybe some of it was the financial stress – who knows? – but we hit a rough patch. Rosemarie and I. We were both drinking too much. Had a really big fight. It was ugly. Like physically violent. Mostly on Rosemarie's part. At one point, I had to push her down because she was swinging for the fences. Hit me straight in the face. Broke my nose. The next day, she said, "I never want to go through that again. We need to break up."

So she took off for a few weeks. Stayed at a friend's house. And then I ran into her in front of the courthouse. I knew she'd be there. Protesting. The protests had to do *with the prosecutor* of the cop who murdered Edson Thevenin. Immediately after the incident, he told the cop: "If you testify in front of a grand jury, I'll give you immunity." So now he was on trial, you know, for prosecutorial misconduct. Bench trial. No jury. And, as you could guess, the judge ruled... not guilty.

I found Rosemarie among the protestors: "Hey, where are you at?" And she was like, "I don't know. I'm sad. Maybe we should try again to make it work?" After that, you know, she moved back into the house. We were unpacking some heavy stuff. Both of us. Just like life experiences that we hadn't been able to share with other partners in the past. It was challenging, sometimes heart-wrenching, but we tried to be supportive of one another. Even if it meant that we settled on some type of untraditional relationship.

One Sunday in early November, we had beautiful weather. I was like, "Hey, you want to have dinner in Providence?" And she was like, "Yeah. Fuck it." So 4:00 in the afternoon, Rosemarie and Waylon and I drove the three hours to Providence. Hit the beach. Swam a little. Got dinner. Drinks. Slept in a tent on a different beach. Woke up before sunrise to a bunch of rowdy ass surfers. Played with the dog. Swam a little more. Jumped in the car and drove home in time for work. We had gone through some shit, you know, so we deserved an adventure.

That *Monday*, Rosemarie received positive test results for COVID and had to isolate for a week. She was fine. And I got tested right away, and somehow it came back negative. That *Tuesday*, though, was Election Day, so Rosemarie wasn't able to vote. She wasn't that bummed. To be honest, I voted, but wasn't that excited about it, either. Obviously, I didn't want the Donald back in office. But I don't really like Old Man Joe or Kamala the Cop. The whole two-party system is fucking ass. In my personal opinion.

*

Something I'll never forget.

When I was set to leave prison, Sandra suggested that I move to Granville with her. Specifically, she said, "Why don't you live here and work in the slate mines?" This random New York town, you know, happens to be like the "Slate Capital of the World." So I said, "Thanks, *mom.*

That's a great way to let me know what you think that I'm worth." Like I've done magical things since I've been home. With my creativity and art and woodwork. But, in her estimation, I should have moved to Granville. Took care of her shitty house. Worked in the fucking mines.

Lately, a lot of my resentment has boiled to the surface. Sandra recently texted, "Oh, I would love for you and Rosemarie to come for lunch." Which is a very bad idea. I used to sometimes think, "Well, she did the best she could." But I don't have that in me anymore. It's a fucking dumpster fire, you know, and you can't look at a dumpster fire and say, "Well, at least we can warm our hands." Some shit is just fucked up. And you have to be honest about that. When I came home, Sandra and I were kind of close, but since then, no, I don't see her – or really any of my siblings – all that much.

I like them well enough, you know, to the degree that you would like anybody that you spent time with at the orphanage. I just don't really fuck with them anymore. I have no idea what Sheri is up to. Couldn't care less. Elizabeth married some seemingly nice enough blue-collar guy. Laura's probably in a home for mentally-challenged adults. Christy actually has some job with the IRS and does very well for herself. Julie: no idea. Minnie moved to Florida and goes by Cynthia now. We're friends on Facebook. I'm friends with Anna on Facebook, too. She's a fucking truck driver!

My youngest brother Kevin just passed away. Like *just* within the last few months. Maybe from COVID? I don't know. Sandra didn't say in her texts. Although, *the last time* she texted me, she wrote: "Say a prayer for your brother." Meaning Mike. Because he got COVID in prison. But I texted her back: "I'm not going to say a prayer. There is no God. And even if there was, he doesn't give a fuck about us. Or he wouldn't let COVID run rampant through our society. Please stop texting me stuff like this. It's idiotic."

And I give her a lot of credit, man. She just responded: "No problem."

Mike's currently in Terra Haute, Indiana, but – before COVID – Sandra said that he was being transferred. This is what she texted then: "Mike is going to be moved soon and has a debt to cover before he leaves for New Jersey. It built up when he first went to Indiana and thought he'd never have a life again. He's regaining some purpose and self-respect, but the debt remains. Is there anyway you can help?" Classic Mike. He cries to Sandra: "Help. They'll kill me if you don't pay." So she sends him money instead of paying her own fucking bills. And then she cries *to me*.

This most recent time, I snapped on her: "He's been doing this for 25 fucking years! And it's your fault, too, because you enable him." I can't deal with it anymore. This might seem shitty of me, but he's been doing this the whole time. Running up debts to buy tobacco and heroin. Getting into fights. He's stabbed people *multiple times* and afterwards said to me: "I didn't have any choice!" I would say, "Mike, I was in the same prison system as you! I know that there are bad, ugly, fucked up situations. But don't get involved. Make better decisions." Tough love.

I did manage to scrape together $50 to send him for Christmas. Of course, the little dickhead never said "thank you." What the fuck? You have COVID! You're in quarantine! You have time to write a letter! Whatever. I didn't even really do it for him. Or Sandra. I sent the money because it sucks being locked up. And a couple of dollars helps *a little bit*, you know what I mean? It's like morphine when you're dying of cancer. Haha. His story is heartbreaking, yeah, but I'm kind of over it. Mike. Sandra. All of them.

I don't feel a lack of family. If you spent five minutes with me in front of my store, you'd see. Half of this town, you know, is like, "Hey Danny! Hey Danny! Hey Danny!" I'm a beloved person with a huge family. My *chosen family*, you know, and your chosen family is almost always better than your random family.

*

That said. Rosemarie was after me to find our more about my birth parents. So we signed onto *ancestry.com*. Did the DNA test.

They send you back a list, you know, hundreds of people who could potentially be my relatives. There was one person who they said was a "close relative." So, one day, while we were watching a movie, Rosemarie did some Facebook research and tracked her down: this 70-year old Black woman from Oklahoma City named Juanita. And... we messaged her. No response. Even attempted to Facebook call her, but she didn't answer. For a while, we didn't hear anything from anyone.

Rosemarie was even more excited about it than me. I was kind of apprehensive. I'm old now. If my birth parents were interested in finding me, then they would've fucking found me already. And then, if I do find them, what if they say, "Leave us alone. We don't want to have anything to do with you." That's a second rejection. So I was playing it cool: "We sent her a message. If she gets back to us, she gets back to us."

And she did get back to us! We even zoomed! Juanita, we're pretty sure, is my aunt. It was a weird feeling, you know, calling her "auntie." She's an artist currently living in Orange County, California. My grandparents, she said, were originally from a small town in Texas, but moved to Oklahoma fleeing racial discrimination. They had their own business for 35 years. Twelve children: nine girls, three boys. Two of those boys are still alive and one passed away. Juanita thinks that the one who died may have been my father. The other two, she's asked if they'll do DNA tests, but they haven't yet responded.

I actually texted Juanita the other day: "Sorry I haven't been more in touch. I'd like to get you know better." Next June, she's going to be a part of a big art show. Maybe I can make it out west for that? And we'll have a loving wonderful reunion, you know, all of that fun happy shit. In the meanwhile, I feel like people think I should be more excited than I am. There's just so much stuff going on. Things to do. Eat, sleep, art, work. Life!

Like I'm super *super* excited about this book that we're writing, but barely even have time to fit this in, you know what I mean?

*

It's funny. I didn't go applying for jobs. This one just fell in my lap. A little trickle of income to keep the bills paid. Ease my financial burden. Until I can figure out what the future looks like for Weathered Wood.

My buddy Marcus. He owns his own commercial construction company. It's just him really. But, late in the summer, he was like, "Danny, I could use some help, but haven't been able to find the right guy. What if I gave you a lot of leeway to do your own work and pay you $25 an hour?" So, every day, I get there at 8:00. We have breakfast. Putz around. Get in the truck. Arrive at a job site by 9:30-10:00. Do a tiny bit of work. Go to the next job site. Do a little more work. Finish up by 2:30-3:00. And then he hands me two $100 bills.

One day, during my first few weeks, I showed up at 8:00. The first hour, as usual, we were sitting around eating egg sandwiches. When Marcus announced, "I think *today* we should smoke weed." So he pulled out a giant blunt and that was the work we attended to. Getting super stoned before going to the job site. And then you should have seen the roof that we were on. On the backside of a two-story house. At the very edge, you know, looking down. Thirty-five feet to the ground. High as fuck.

I've known Marcus for years. We met through another friend when I first moved to Troy. He's a good dude with a good heart. But he's also going through some emotional shit at the moment. He used to have a long-term cocaine and alcohol problem, you know, seven grams of cocaine every day and then a bottle of alcohol at night to come down. He did this for two and a half years. Running his company the whole time.

Finally, he decided to stop doing *that*, you know, and spent $6,000 to have an ayahuasca medicine trip in South America. And now he's obsessed with psychedelics. He's serious, serious, serious about his psychedelic mushrooms. One morning, he invited me into his house to show off all of these different packages. They were only a couple of ounces each, but all different strains. He said, "I just took a gram of this super powerful strain." Pointing to one labeled Penis Envy. It's hilarious, man, to be at work, and *your boss* is tripping on mushrooms.

Do you want to hear a crazy story? So Marcus loves having me around and treats me pretty well. At the same time, I don't love working for someone else. I'm grateful for the extra cash, but it's not really what I want to be doing. And, occasionally, I'll get frustrated when he's not efficient with my time. For instance. Marcus brought me along to a job that he *might* do. I didn't need to be there. But, because I'm a good employee, if he's talking to a client, then I'll make myself useful. Organize materials. Clean out the truck.

Okay. We were downtown Troy outside of I Love Pizza. While Marcus talked with the owner about a leaky roof, I cleaned out the back of the truck. Threw out the old coffee cups and sandwich wrappers. And when he was ready, we drove over to a job site to do a gutter job. Usually, it's super simple. You show up. Take a measurement. Make the gutter. Put the gutter on the house. And leave. However, the previous week, a client had picked the wrong color and shut us down. When we returned a few days later, the client wasn't home. So, this particular day, we were back. For the third time. Determined to finish this job.

We parked. Went around to the back of the truck to get some materials. And Marcus looked up: "Hmmmm. Did you happen see a plastic bag back here?" I said, "I don't know, man. There was *a lot* of trash. I threw it all away." He started to panic: "Oh my god! Oh my god!" I was like, "What? What was in the bag?" And he yelled, "A quarter pound of fucking psychedelic mushrooms!" That I had thrown into a random garbage can. On a city street in Troy. And now we were in Niskayuna. Twenty-five minutes away.

So he was totally freaking out. I was like, "Listen, motherfucker. This is your own fault. I was trying to be helpful while you were wasting my time. Next time you have mushrooms just laying around in the truck, maybe mention it to a nigga. Let him know, hey, BY THE WAY..." He was like, "I'm not mad. I'm not mad." But now we were *dangerously* racing back from Niskayuna. I thought he was going to flip the truck.

I called Rosemarie: "Hey, where are you at?" And she just happened to be *on the same block* where we had been that morning. I was like, "Uh. Could you possibly... look through the garbage cans on that street?" She was like, "What? No. I have to meet a client for a haircut." I begged her: "Please! It's really important." So she sent a couple of pictures of the trashcans on that street. And sure enough, there, in one of the pictures, sitting on top of the trash, I saw the bag of mushrooms. After Rosemarie retrieved the bag, she texted, "Tell your boss to stop pissing his pants. I found his drugs."

We ran into Weathered Wood right as her client was walking in. And she said, "Hey, guys. Your, uh, package is right over there."

*

The day before the storm, I was so busy. Running around and running around. It was past 8:00 when I finally got home, you know, and went straight to bed. Anyway, I had heard that we were only getting six inches. So when I woke up the next morning and saw *two feet of snow,* it was like, "Shit. I wish I had prepared a little more."

It took us half an hour to shovel out the van. And then Rosemarie got in and… towed me along on my snowboard. I held onto a long rope. As she drove 10, 15, 20 mph. It's somewhere between surfing, snowboarding, and water skiing. You start in the middle of the road, but as you pick up speed, you can glide over to one side and hop up onto the snowbank. And then you're just three feet off of the ground. Floating in fresh powder.

We went back and forth a few times. Not our street. One street over, they built this mile-long access road for the giant trucks that frequent the area. But they weren't running any trucks that day, so there was no traffic at all. Rosemarie got a video where you can see me surfing the snowbank in the passenger side window. Although when she got to the end of the road, she took the corner at like 15 mph. And it was icy, you know, so the van just started spinning sideways. On the video, you can hear her screaming – and laughing – "Oh no! Oh no! Oh no!"

It was so much fun. I played in the snow *all day*. After the tow-behind, Rosemarie was not as enthusiastic as I was about playing in the snow. She went home to watch Netflix, and I ran out to build a jump. Because you don't get *this much* snow very often. So when it happens, you have to capitalize. Listen, man. If I have an opportunity to jump 20 feet through the air on my snowboard, then you can bet that I'm going to take it.

So I went over to RPI. The college "up the hill" in Troy. There's an amazing spot near the bottom of the campus. *The last time* I was there, though, I spent a whole day building this huge jump. Shoveled and shaped it and shoveled and shaped it. The sun went down, and it still wasn't ready yet. So I left and came back the next morning to put on the finishing touches. But when I got there... RPI maintenance was on top with shovels. I was like, "Hey! What the fuck are you doing?" And they were like, "Sorry. The Head of Operations says it's not allowed anymore. Too dangerous." Motherfuckers!

But, this day in December, I took my chances. Long shot. I thought, "It's the best spot in the area. Maybe, because of COVID, they won't have the staffing to deal with it." And I was right. No one was around. I barely finished the jump before sundown, but did get to hit it a couple of times. I also called my friend Christian, who snowboards, and he came by to hit the jump. And took a video of me to post on Instagram.

That next day was Saturday. December 18th. My birthday! I turned 50 years old! All I wanted to do was play around on the jump. Rosemarie didn't want to come, but I did get to hang out with my daughter. I had just found her a new snowboard, barely used, *by a dumpster*. Perfect-sized for Reilley. She didn't hit the jump, no, but she does have crazy balls! Bends her knees, points her nose straight down the hill, and... there she goes! I was like, "Dude, you have to learn how to stop, too. Your only plan can't be go fast and fall down." But she'll learn. It just takes practice.

And then, that night, I was part of a little art show at a bar. Rosemarie, once again, didn't come because we were in the middle of a big fight. Only a couple of people showed. My boss Marcus and his wife. This woman Suzy, who makes macramé work that I sell in my store, and her husband. We social-distanced and wore masks, but the place was empty. Rare Form Brewing. I've been friends with the owner, Kevin, for a long time. We play basketball together with some other local business owners. Although with COVID, you know, we're all doing bad business-wise. And not playing any basketball, either.

What were Rosemarie and I fighting about? Oh, we're always fighting. I was really sad that she didn't want to come out on my birthday *at all*. She said to me: "No. I didn't want to go and take pictures of you hitting the jump. I don't want to be your cheerleader." I was like, "Damn, dude. I don't want a cheerleader. I just want *a friend*." And she was like, "How dare you!" And I was like, "How dare I what? Be heartbroken?" I was literally crying: "We can't keep doing this."

So she moved out again that following Monday. Needed some space. Found her own place, you know, but also needed me to help her move in. Who the fuck else was she going to ask? I have a perfect moving van. Whatever. I said, "Okay. You're a fucking asshole! But c'mon. I'll help you move."

*

Yesterday, I saw an AARP commercial asking, "Are you 50 or older?" And I said to the TV: "Yes I am!" I'm now in some whole other category, man. When COVID's over, you know, I'm going to be so nasty in the 50+ basketball leagues. I'll fuck those cats up.

But it's official. I'm an old man. Like I was over at Krystal's to spend Christmas with Reilley. And Krystal's been trying to get Reilley to not talk back as much. And I don't yell at my daughter. Would never *ever* spank her. Put my hands on her. Use any kind of violence. However... we were both telling Reilley, you know, *when we were growing up,* you didn't talk back to your parents. Because you might get punched in the fucking face. Which, I know, is very 50-year old man behavior. This is how it was, kid, *back in the day*.

I go over to Krystal's every year for Christmas. Watch Reilley open her presents. Oh my god. She's *obsessed* with something called Roblox. Like we'll be hanging out, and she'll play Roblox on her phone the whole time. I'll say to her: "Hey, enough already. Put the phone down for like five minutes. Please." But Christmas was fun. I called her outside: "Come here." She never stops bugging her mom for money, so I gave her a $100 bill on the sneak. She gasped, "Ohhhhh."

Reilley *gave me* a new hat. One of those warm hunting caps. With the flaps that come down over the ears. That was the only Christmas present I received from anyone. No, wait, Rosemarie bought me a stationary bike. I was like, "Have you ever heard me say that I wanted a stationary bike?" I hate stationary bikes! I get most of my cardio from running. You have to take care of the ticker, you know what I mean? I usually do alternate days, two miles, pretty consistently. But lately I've been struggling with pain in my hip, I think, from overpronating.

Rosemarie was like, "I thought... because you haven't been able to run..." And I was like, "I know. I love you. It's an awesome idea. But when you spend that much money, maybe check if it's something that the person really wants!" She was tight with me: "Well, I wish you would have told me *before I took it out of the box.*" I didn't want to hurt her feelings. So I actually tried to ride it. A couple of times. But it's just too awkward for me, you know, so now it's in her apartment.

We didn't see each other on New Year's. I didn't do anything. Read a little. Went to bed early. Super low-key. Unlike last year when we went to Philadelphia. I had built a table for a customer in Philly, but there was a little problem in one of the seams. So, New Year's Eve, Rosemarie and I drove down. Fixed the table. And then went to see one of my favorite bands, Clutch, at Union Transfer. They played *Blast Tyrant*, my favorite album, *in its entirety*. Totally insane. It was the first time Rosemarie had ever been in a mosh pit.

That was also the night when I started drinking again. After many, many, years sober. 2020 was definitely a good year to be drinking. Fuck yeah. But after New Year's, this year, I decided to stop drinking again. Yeah, I'm over two weeks sober and pretty happy about it. I've already done more around the house in two weeks than I did all of last year!

*

I worked New Year's Day. For two hours, 10:00 to noon, and made $300. It was a holiday, I guess, so Marcus gave me a holiday bonus. I was like, "Alright. Fine with me!"

Before work, I went to Home Depot to buy spray paint. I mostly gesso my boards, you know, paint them all white. And then work them over with red, yellow, and blue. But I shared some pics with my old art teacher Jeff, and he was like, "What's with you and primary colors?" So, at Home Depot, I found a really mossy green. Since then, I've been painting the primary colors on top of this darker green background. For a totally different effect.

Jeff critiques my work a lot. In the way that he wants me to grow as an artist. Always constructive. But that's been our relationship for years now. I want him to tell me how great my work is, and he'll be like, "I don't know. Meh." Although I feel the same way about his music. He actually has some new stuff coming out soon! During the pandemic, he said, his new band Famous Problems wrote 13 new songs and cut a record. I'm super excited to tell him how much I hate it. Haha.

I love that man. We've been talking lately. About seeing if this organization called Community Partners Action might sponsor me, you know, to start a prison art program at the Rensselaer County Jail. I don't know how or when. There are so many things on my agenda right now. More shit to accomplish than I have life to live. But I would love to do it. I have such a huge appreciation for the program. So many fond memories.

Speaking of memories. Guess who I ran into buying paint at Home Depot? Hezzie. The director of the CAC. She spends a lot of time in Italy now, so I hadn't seen her in a long time. I can't believe it's been so long *since I worked there*. Making the original designs, you know, that I now sell in my store. The years go by too fast, man! She actually said, "Hey, I heard that Weathered Wood might close. Let me know if there's anything I can do." And I said, 'No, no, no. Don't worry, Hezzie. We're figuring it out."

And then, *when I was leaving the store*, guess who was walking out at the same time? Kate. My ex. We both had masks on, yeah, but you can recognize someone who you know that well. She said, "Hey! I'm going out to my car. To take a break." And I asked, "Can I walk with you? Shoot the shit?" She had been waitressing at a restaurant, you know, until that whole industry got hammered by COVID. So now she's back at Home Depot. It was nice to catch up. Not contentious at all. My boss Marcus – who knew Kate – he was like, "So... now that you're single?" And I was like, "Fuck no! She's *crazy*."

After work, I went and hung one of my paintings at Placid Baker. This awesome little bakery around the corner from my store. I sold the painting dirt cheap. The owner loves it. Tom. We've been friends for a while. I've done a few handyman projects for him in the past. Tom used to be a guitar player in the Troy hardcore scene. And whenever I go in there to do anything, he's always blasting hardcore. That day, while I installed the painting, he was listening to God Forbid. Do you know that band? Look them up!

They put my painting in a fucking prime spot. Right by the counter. It's a small space, you now, so now, when you're ordering your almond croissant, my painting will be all up in your face. Over the summer, when I was painting out in the middle of the street, sometimes people would come up and talk to me. Well, when I wasn't paying attention, a feather must have blown onto this canvas. And I just painted over it. You can still see the outline. It's so cool. One of my favorite paintings ever.

My favorite *favorite* paintings are ones that I did at Osborn. Giant abstract landscapes filled with weird-ass figures, part octopus, part machine. After prison, Damien came to visit once and asked, "What ever happened to those paintings you made in prison?" I pointed to a pile on the floor. He was like, "They're just lying there! Let me take them back to Sacramento and hang them in my house." I just messaged him last month on Facebook: "Hey, do you still have my paintings?" And he did! Even promised to send them back *by Christmas*. Swore up and down.

So I messaged him again the other day, "Where are my paintings, asshole? I can't wait to see you again. And brutally beat you within an inch of your life." And he wrote back, "Haha. You're not that tough." We went back and forth like that. Although he also said shit like, "I still love you like a brother, man. It's sad the way things turned out." I tried to tell him: "Yo, it's not that sensitive. Just pay me the fucking money you owe me." But then I made a joke, too, you know, about us smashing through the prison walls with runaway laundry carts. Which we both thought was fucking hilarious.

*

I'm really fucking excited.

When they sent me away, and I told people my bank robbing stories, even the other prisoners would say, "Whoa! You should write a book about that shit." And then, after prison, whenever I tell civilians, they always say, "Whoa! You should write a book about that shit." And now that it's finally becoming a reality, so much more has happened in my life. I'm not only defined by bank robbing, but also by the things that I've done since. This book is now about a guy *who happened to rob some banks*.

The process has been harder than I expected. Digging through my memory. Laying everything out. It's work, man. That's all I can say. Some of this stuff, when I look back, it's like, "Holy shit!" I don't want to think about that anymore. I almost don't care to tell these stories. Even my favorites. I've told them *so many times*. It's easy to forget. That they're more than stories. That this is my real life.

Don't get me wrong. I don't have a sense of shame about committing crimes. My moral compass might be off. I know that there are people out there – and you could potentially fall into this category? – who are very serious about following the rules. We have rules for a reason, and if they're not followed, then society will descend into chaos. Eh. I don't agree with that sentiment. Because the whole system is criminal. These people running the show: they're fucking psychopaths! Committing crimes upon crimes. Over and over. All of the time. And getting away with everything.

Being a bank robber is definitely a part of who I am. And more important to me now than ever. It was largely fueled by – although I didn't have the term for it then – my fight against systemic racism. How the system itself is built to limit possibilities for Black and Brown and poor people. Sure, I was in a crazy state of mind. Where I looked at the future and saw myself being nothing but a wage slave. And I didn't want to accept that. Luckily, I've been able to carve out a living doing something I love. But that's what it was all about then. Rebellion against misery and sorrow.

Obviously, you can look back and think, "Damn." If I had just paid a little more attention in school. If I had been more serious about sports, you know, maybe my life would have turned out very differently. There's that mental game that you can play, but you can't ever go back and change anything. So what's the point? Could I have been in a different position today if I hadn't robbed banks? Of course! But regret is just wasted energy, don't you think?

And maybe rebellion was just in my DNA? Or maybe I was a "good" kid until I found out that I was adopted and that triggered something? Whatever the case, I've always been super rebellious. But, hey, some of the greatest leaders throughout history have been rebellious. The founding founders of this country, you know, were rebelling against the tyranny of Britain. It's true. Say what you will about those colonial slave-owning motherfuckers, they certainly knew how to riot. We've all learned that from *Hamilton*, right? Not that I've seen it. I don't have Disney+.

How about, last week, our founding fathers' racist ancestors rioting in DC? I knew that was going to be a shitshow. It had just been building up the whole year, you know what I mean? So I expected it to be insane. And it was *insane*. Senators fleeing. This mob. Successfully whipped up into a fervor! Storming the fucking capitol of the United States! And convinced en masse that they were acting in service to their great leader. Who would, without question, have their backs. Well, guess what? He didn't! He doesn't!

I think it's poetic justice. The guy that was in Nancy Pelosi's office. Holding up her mail and shit. You're going to prison! And whose fault is that? It's yours! Because you're stupid as fuck! There's going to be hundreds of these idiots getting locked up. And I hope they stay locked up for a long time. Oh yeah. Put a bunch of white boys in prison for a change! Here's your fucking orange jumpsuit. Here's your fucking bedroll. Here's your fucking dirty-ass prison cell. Get in. Good luck.

Let me tell you. If I was in DC that day, and of a previous mindset, I would have got myself a motorcycle. And with everyone distracted, you know, gone and robbed some banks. Five in a row. From one to the next. Boom! Boom! Boom! "Give me the money! Give me the money! Give me the money!" Now I don't suggest robbing banks anymore, no, but hey, if you want to talk about how someone *might* rob a bank *if they wanted to,* I'd be happy to have a conversation over a cup of coffee.

SOUNDTRACK

"Freedom" – Rage Against the Machine
"Stairway to Heaven" – Led Zeppelin
"Bring the Noise" – Anthrax ft. Public Enemy
"Caught Up in You" – 38 Special
"Working Class Hero" – John Lennon / Screaming Trees
"How Will I Laugh Tomorrow" – Suicidal Tendencies
"1st of Tha Month" – Bone Thugs-N-Harmony
"Congratulations Asshole" – Congratulations Asshole
"Flesh Shapes the Day" – Tom Morello
"Fortunate Son" – CCR / Clutch
"Bankrobber" – The Clash

&

"Rob a Bank" – The Butterflies of Love

NOTES

The contents of this book are Daniel Killion's personal memoirs of how he experienced and interpreted the events detailed in this book. They are in no way meant to be a historical accounting. The thoughts, opinions and recollections in no way reflect the opinions of Matthew Klane or the publisher. This book is intended purely for entertainment purposes.

*

Matthew Klane is a writer and artist living in Albany, NY. A previous long-form single-subject "Voice Portrait," *Portrait: 40 Years in Porn* with his uncle David Christopher, was also published by Volossal in 2020. You can find links to more of his art and writing at **www.matthewklane.com**.

*

The introduction to this book, "Protest Central", was previously published online by the *Coal Hill Review*. Many thanks to those editors. If you would like to learn more about or browse artwork by Danny Killion, you can visit **www.weatheredwoodtroy.com** or find him on Instagram **@weatheredwoodtroy**.

*

Community Partners in Action supports the transition from life in the prison system to life in the community. Their model for impact blends direct services, community action, and restorative justice advocacy. Over the past decade, they've worked to make important gains toward ending mass incarceration in Connecticut. To learn more, go to **www.cpa-ct.org**.

*

Finally, if you would like to support Troy 4 Black Lives in calling "for a measurable commitment to police accountability and justice that protects the citizens, visitors, and neighbors of Troy, NY," then please consider donating at **www.troy4blacklives.com**.